DISCUSSION PARTNER

A Radical Transformation to Unrivaled Service in the Insurance Industry

TROY KORSGADEN

COURSE MANUAL

Discussion Partner: Course Manual
by Troy Korsgaden

ISBN: 978-1-950718-48-1

Printed in the United States of America

Discussion Partner is available in Amazon Kindle, Barnes & Noble Nook and Apple iBooks.

Contents

Module 4: Power Position

Module 5: Marketing and Lead Development

Module 6: The Customer Journey

Module 7: Closing and Follow-Up

Module 8: A New Normal

Module 1: Developing a Strategy

introduction

Becoming a Discussion Partner

Thank you for taking the time to join me in examining what it means to become a Discussion Partner operation. What do I mean by "Discussion Partner"?

The world has rapidly changed over the past decade—we can see it happening all around us. The consumer has taken control of their buying patterns across all industries. Retail was the first to become affected by this paradigm shift. However, no industry is immune to the encroachment that digital services have on their customer base. And, although we must deal with the reality that digital based purchasing is the "new normal," we should not fear it, for it will never take the place of what a human can offer: a relationship based on trust, guidance and transparency—a relationship built on the Discussion Partner Model.

DISCUSSION PARTNER

To thrive in in today's environment, it's necessary that we move our firms from a transactional model in business into a Discussion Partner Model. The nature of our business will always require transactional services. However, we need to change the perspective of what our clients see in "the front of the house" versus what we do in "the back of the house." Don't assume your customer knows what you're doing for them. Transparency goes a long way in building trust and forming lasting relationships with your clients.

To thrive in in today's environment, it's necessary that we move our firms from a transactional model in business into a Discussion Partner Model.

We're moving from a transactional model in business into a Discussion Partner Model. Today, people buy from those they know and trust. They do more business with someone they think of as a Discussion Partner. A Discussion Partner is someone they can come to for guidance and advice without the threat of being "sold" something. In a couple of clicks, anyone can find anything they want to know about insurance—even your client. Deciphering all of that information is daunting, even for a professional like you. Today's customer is not coming to you for information they can easily access;

instead, they're coming to you for expert advice, opinions, and recommendations based on their individual needs. They are coming to you for an open dialogue, because you're their Discussion Partner.

In this manual, we'll explore how you can become that partner for them. I will teach you how to set up systems and processes to ensure that you have a 360-degree view of the customer. The days of canned quoting are over. Now, we need to get to know our clients even more deeply than before. We need to know everything we can about both their professional and personal lives. The more we know, the more effectively we can help our clients. Your customers desire and expect great service; you have the potential to be their gateway to all things insurance and financial services. You're their starting point.

This manual was designed to ask thought-provoking questions about your business and provide you with actionable items to begin making changes from Day One. There are no right or wrong answers. In fact, the way you answer these questions today will most certainly not be the way you'll answer in six months, a year, or even five years from now. I recommended not biting off more than you can chew. We've all fallen into the trap of getting overly excited and trying to change everything all at once. Take your time and implement ideas and suggestions only as you can effectively execute them. There's no set time to get them all done. It's more important that you begin!

Join me, and we'll change how we do business from the ground up. Why? Because we want to create a seamless ecosystem for those we serve. We're going to put the customer first in everything we do. And when we do, we will watch our businesses thrive and grow like never before!

Takeaway Questions:

1. What procedures are present in your organization that fall under a transactional organizational model (i.e. quoting, vehicle changes, updating addresses/phone numbers, etc.)?

____

____

____

____

____

2. What's one thing you can do this week in your daily operations to begin putting the customer first (i.e. calling to say, "thank you", offering after-hours contact information, etc.)?

____

____

____

____

____

Actionable Item: Copy and paste the following onto your calendar!

Subject: Becoming a Discussion Partner: Transactional Processes

Time Frame: 15 minutes

Notes: Start a list of any/all current processes in your office today that fall under a transactional sales/service model.

Next Steps: Begin outlining how to change these transactional processes to fit under the Discussion Partner Model. The goal is to make every interaction with your customer more meaningful.

How to Create Actionable Calendar Items

1. Keep it short – block in fifteen-minute increments.
2. Never remove an item until it is completed!

Example:

Subject: Roadmap: search web for templates that pertain to your industry of business

Time Frame: 15 minutes

Notes: Find templates and examples to facilitate creating a personalized roadmap for my business.

How to Follow-Up:

1. Determine the next date to "touch" the event. This is what keeps your project moving forward.

2. Change the due date in your calendar item to that date.
3. Update subject as needed.
4. Add notes each time you work on the event to include the date and a brief summary of what you accomplished. These notes will be extremely useful as you move forward. They will allow you to track your progress, and effectively catalogue your workflow.

The key is to continue moving the event forward in an organized, effective manner until completion. Keeping the scope to fifteen-minute increments will ensure that the task does not become daunting, thus increasing the odds that it will be completed.

session 1

Getting a Grip on Time

We all have twenty-four hours in a day, so being a student of your time is very important. Today, I'm in my fifties, and I realize the value of my time more now than I did when I was twenty-five. I block time for myself personally, for my health, for my business, and for my family. It doesn't matter whether you work for a carrier, whether you're a consultant like me, or whether you own an agency or firm: you need to block time in all these areas. Get a grip on time. If you don't, it will get away from you.

I like to be "flexible like a reed, not rigid like an oak," as the saying goes. I plan my day in advance, but I'm also flexible, and I keep moving. I'll go outside of my plan and come back to it when necessary. I know what I want to accomplish, but I'm okay with the fact that not every minute of the day goes as planned.

I plan my day in advance, but I'm also flexible, and I keep moving. No matter what you do or what your position, your health is important. I didn't take this seriously when I was younger. Block time for health. Maybe you need to walk; maybe you need to simply sit, like I do, three times a day, and be quiet for a little while.

I plan my day in advance, but I'm also flexible, and I keep moving.

All of this makes a difference in your performance and in the way you work. By blocking time, you allow yourself to think about what's important, so that you can move toward those things. For me, being a student of time is very important. I'm not perfect at it, but I'm getting better every day. Progress is what's important to me—I don't want to go backwards; I want to keep moving forwards. So, I focus on using my time wisely, and focus on getting the most out of every minute, hour, and day.

Practical Application: Log and Control Technology Use

I've learned this tip recently, and it's made a dramatic difference in the way I use my time: I limit how much I use my digital device. Let's admit it—we're all addicted to it. We need it, right? I'm not going to cut it all the way out, because it helps me in my business, my friendships, and my family.

However, I've got to be honest with myself. I started journaling how much time I spent using my technology, and what I was using it for. This helped me set some limits for myself. I don't look at my device during the first hour I'm awake every day. I also don't look at it during lunch, unless I'm expecting something very important to happen—and I know that in advance. It's the same thing at dinner—we've all been to a dinner where everyone's on their phones.

As I started to log my time, it helped me realize that I need to shut off my technology more often. I need to be in control of how I use my time—not have it control me.

Takeaway Questions:

1. Are you more of a rigid planner, or someone who is flexible and "goes with the flow"? How can you develop the quality that you're not as strong in?

____

____

____

____

____

2. For one week, journal or log the time you spend on your electronic devices. Can you identify some ways this use is affecting your workday, mentality, relationships, stress levels, and productivity (for better or worse)?

3. Spend time creating a system to plan your day, week, month and year in advance.

Actionable Item: Copy and paste the following onto your calendar!

Subject: Getting a Grip on Time: Review Your Time

Time Frame: 15 minutes

Notes: Review your schedule over the last week, month, six months, and beyond. What is the majority of your time being spent on? What takes up most of your day? Are these items scheduled or not scheduled?

Next Steps: Create a framework to move toward a more "balanced" day.

session 2

Staying Focused

Staying focused is a big subject for leaders and business owners. It doesn't matter what your position is—it's difficult for all of us to stay focused. There are so many things fighting for our mind space: news, advertising, radio, social media... the barrage of information and attention-grabbing content is endless.

Everybody wants a piece of your time and attention. Stay focused. How? I learned something a long time ago at a conference. I was waiting to go up and speak. A gentleman nearby said, "I want you to write this down— 'The Law of Seventy-Two.' Here it is: When you get information, you must take action on it within seventy-two hours. If you don't, you're never going to take action on it."

I wrote that down that day; and it changed my life! Now, when I see a good idea, concept, or system, I block time to consider it. I literally put it on my schedule within seventy-two hours! I think about if that idea is *truly* important to implement.

When you get information, you must take action on it within seventy-two hours. Let's say that I hear about an excellent model for a review program, and I want to consider implementing it into my business. I'm first going to block time to examine the program—even if it's only fifteen minutes. During those fifteen minutes, I'm not going to do anything except think about that idea. This way, I can place it forward on the calendar for another block of time. I keep it on the calendar, and I keep thinking about it, until I start to develop an execution plan. My plan goes onto the calendar, and I begin to execute.

When you get information, you must take action on it within seventy-two hours.

I can afford fifteen minutes a day to think about issues and ideas. Sometimes, I'll be able to knock them off my calendar completely. The point I want you to see here is that you don't need to blow up your business in order to transform it. Think about things in small chunks and keep moving them forward until you execute them. Inspect what you expect to make sure that those processes are sustainable. In the next section, I will explain how to utilize a consistent calendar system.

Practical Application: Have a Discussion Partner

Do you have a mentor or a coach? If you want to be a good Discussion Partner, you need someone to talk to in order to ensure you're doing the right things. I have mentors in many different areas of my life. To stay focused, find someone you know who is also focused. Ask them to be your Discussion Partner on a specific subject. Buy them lunch and have a discussion—it's a wonderful opportunity for both of you.

Takeaway Questions:

1. Does your current schedule have room for a few of these fifteen-minute time blocks per day? If not, what you can move around to make it work?

____

____

____

____

____

2. What's one development, idea, or possibility you want to block time to consider this week? Why is this idea potentially important or even essential to your organization?

____

____

DISCUSSION PARTNER

____

____

____

Actionable Item: Copy and paste the following onto your calendar!

Subject: Staying Focused: Determine 3–5 Possible Mentors/Coaches

Time Frame: 15 minutes

Notes: Create a list of three to five possible mentors/coaches to contact and look for synergies, compatibility, and willingness to take on this role. Include reasons why this person would be a good fit for your personal and business development.

Next Steps: Begin making the initial contact and setting formal meeting to collaborate and discuss what you hope to gain from the relationship.

session 3

The Importance of Strategy

Let's set the framework for the strategy we're going to use as we move forward. It's important to have a strong foundation—I often refer to this as creating a roadmap to your future. When architects design a large building, they dig the foundation down deep. You don't want to simply breeze over your strategy. It's worth the time and the effort it takes to do it correctly. But remember, this can be built upon over time in small amounts. The deeper the foundation, the higher the building.

Remember, I like to block fifteen-minute units where I can think and execute. Don't be afraid to block time for your strategy 2-3 times a day, if that's what you need! A roadmap to your future is essential. Architects don't operate spontaneously. They don't say, "We'll start at ground level and build as we go. We'll see what happens from there and figure it out." No! They file a design plan, make sure it's up to code, and consult with several different officials to get clearance for it.

The deeper the foundation, the higher the building will be.

The deeper the foundation, the higher the building will be. Then, later, if circumstances dictate the need for a change, they'll be able to do so wisely because they filed their plan initially. A plan empowers you to know your endgame—your finish line. Your strategy doesn't need to be perfect; it simply needs to give you a direction—a foundation off of which to work.

Let's work together to put that plan into place now.

Practical Application: Create a Roadmap

Don't try to recreate the wheel. There are unlimited examples, templates and recommendations that are available online. Take advantage of these free samples to assist with designing your own personal plan. Remember, this is a work in progress. The key is to start! You will add, change and delete as you begin to tailor your personal roadmap to the future based on your needs, and the needs of your business.

Takeaway Questions:

1. Do you currently block your time throughout the day for appointments and tasks? If you are not including tasks, do you find that most of your tasks are not getting done?

____

____

____

____

____

2. What's one strategic question or goal that you can schedule time to think about this week?

____

____

____

____

____

Actionable Item: Copy and paste the following onto your calendar!

Subject: The Importance of Strategy: List all Appointments and Tasks for This Week

Time Frame: 15 minutes

Notes: Block all appointments and begin adding tasks to calendar in fifteen-minute increments, or blocks.

Next Steps: Continue to add all appointments and tasks to calendar. Take time to audit your calendar to ensure your time is being spent in the most productive ways.

session 4

Goal Setting

In my book, *Power Position Your Agency,* I spend a lot of time talking about goals. I still feel that goal setting is very important; but my view of goals back then and my view on goals now has changed slightly.

Today, I'm more interested in the reason for the goal than the goal itself. Don't get me wrong–I believe in the law of attraction; I believe in getting what you want. And I don't set ridiculous expectations; but there are certain things I want. I set them out on pen and paper as goals (today, I put them in a device. If you look at my phone, it's populated with my top five goals). These goals are important to me. Every time I look at them, I get reinvigorated to go after them.

I'm more interested in the reason for the goal than the goal itself. In the book, I talk about building your goals today on what you want tomorrow. As I think about what I want, I'm going to move towards it. But I have to have the right reasons;

that's the slight change that has powered everything for me. All the mentors I work with, and all the people that influence my life—through books, audio, and anything I'm learning from—will tell you that your reasons are the power behind your goals.

I'm more interested in the reason for the goal than the goal itself.

My biggest goal for my business today is to effectively serve my clients. Whether I own an agency, own a firm, or lead a carrier operation, I want to put the customer first. Everything flows from there. Why? Because if I give the client the service they desire and have every right to expect, I reach my goal.

How do I do this? By focusing on my reasons for why. If I have enough reasons why, I can do anything. I can put a man on the moon if I have enough reasons—we proved that, right? There are some audacious goals out there; and people are achieving them because they believe, and because they have enough reasons to get there.

Practical Application: List the Reasons Behind Your Goal

If you have a goal—let's just say it's to put on someone to help you with life insurance—you've got to sit down and say, "If I'm going to bring somebody on and make them a profit center, I've got to have enough reasons. Why do I want to hire and develop a life expert in my operation?" Start to list the reasons behind your goal. Figure out what you want and write the reasons why. You'll find yourself closer and closer to that goal, until you've finally achieved it.

Takeaway Questions:

1. Think about your number one goal for your organization at the moment. What's your motivation for setting that goal?

____

____

____

____

____

2. Be honest with yourself—if you listed out your motivations, where on that list would serving your customer be? Would it fall at #1 on the list? #3? #10?

____

____

____

____

____

3. I keep my goals as the home screen on my phone so that I constantly am reminded of them. Do you have your goals in a place that you can see them all throughout the day? If not, where can you put them where you do see them every day?

___

___

___

___

___

Actionable Item: Copy and paste the following onto your calendar!

Subject: Goalsetting: Make a List of all Goals for Your Personal and Professional Life

Time Frame: 15 minutes

Notes: Get creative – this will be narrowed down moving forward.

Next Steps: Pick your top five goals and write out the reasons "why" you chose each of them.

session 5

Be a Student of Your Business

What are the implications of what we've talked about so far? Your organization needs to be effective. When we hire staff, everybody on our team has to be a profit center. If they're not, they're a cost center—and we can't afford cost centers.

It doesn't matter what your revenue is, or the size of your organization—if your staff isn't bringing in profit, you can't afford them. Likewise, if *you're* not a profit center, they can't afford *you*. One of the things we constantly need to do is look for efficiencies. Just because we did it back in the eighties doesn't mean it works today; just because we did it two years ago doesn't mean it works today.

The people gaining market share in our business are creating efficiencies every day. We study these people, and you need to do so, too! Learn from what they're doing—from the way they answer phones to how they follow up to the way they ask questions.

Just because we did it back in the eighties doesn't mean it works today; just because we did it two years ago doesn't mean it works today.

If you want to be efficient, be a student of your business. Study the services you give; the products you provide; the way they are delivered. Are these things done in a timely fashion? Are you getting back to people? Be a student of what you do.

By getting better, you will earn the right to put more products and services into every household and business you serve. You're not going to sell every time you offer; but be transparent, and you'll build trust, whether they buy or not.

Practical Application: Spend a Day with Your Staff

If you want to make sure your team is comprised of profit centers, spend a day with each of them. It's not as easy as you think. Listen first—don't instruct. Then, you can take them into a safe place and train them.

Spend a day with one of your team members, cataloguing everything they do and say. Then, sit down with them, mentor them, give them advice, and develop them.

You each get paid for the value you bring—not just the hours you work.

Takeaway Questions:

1. Do you have processes and procedures in place to evaluate whether your team members are profit centers? If not, do you know where to get measuring tools? Are you consistent with measuring/analytics?

____

____

____

____

____

2. Who is the first team member you want to sit down with? Make an appointment with yourself today to set this meeting, and plan below for the things you want to talk about.

____

____

____

____

____

Actionable Item: Copy and paste the following onto your calendar!

Subject: Be a Student of Your Business: Profit Centers vs. Cost Centers

Time Frame: 15 minutes

Notes: List your employees in order of who you currently feel is the strongest to the weakest. List the reasons why you feel this way.

Next Steps: Starting with the strongest on your list, think about what attributes they possess that make them a "Profit Center" for your business. How can you immediately encourage all of your employees to emulate them?

session 6

Be Busy Being Born

I love this line by Bob Dylan: "He not busy being born is busy dying." I watch so many people in our industry—and others—waiting for things to go back to the way they used to be. There are certain fundamentals that don't change; but life is changing all around us.

Have you ever heard the saying, "Progress is the secret to success"? To have progress, we need to continually retool and be reborn. We need to be on a quest to learn. Never stop learning. Remember to block time to learn. When I get up in the morning, I've learned not to look at my phone for the first hour I'm awake. I have certain things I do in that hour of quiet; one of them is learning.

The best way to be busy being born is to focus on where you are right now. Don't fret about where you were, or where you think you should be. Look at the way forward, and how you can progress every day.

How can you improve your business? How can you better serve your team? How can you better serve your clients? How can you improve your technology? Your systems? Your customer service? How can you be a better Discussion Partner? As you think about these things, you'll naturally begin to look for information, in all kinds of places, that will help you answer these questions. I'm constantly looking for books to read on a multitude of subjects. It's so important to be an expert and develop yourself in areas in which you're not an expert.

The best way to be busy being born is to focus on where you are right now.

Growing is one of the most important things you'll ever do in this business. Whether you're just now entering into the industry, or whether you've spent a lifetime in it, this is an essential skill. After all, one day, when you look back and turn the lights out, you want to be able to say to yourself, "I was busy being born every day I was in this business."

Practical Application: Be Around the Right People

You've heard this a million times—that's because it's true. Who you surround yourself with will determine who you become. Jim Rohn asks, "Have you stopped recently and taken an inventory of who you're around? What do they have you thinking? What have they got you saying? What have they got you doing?"

What do they have you becoming? Constantly be assessing who you're around in the context of who you want to become.

Takeaway Questions:

1. What are you learning about today? This week? How are you growing your mind right now?

____

____

____

____

____

2. What are three to five things you could change to "be busy being born"? It could be blocking your day, listening to a new podcast or audiobook, attending a conference or seminar, etc.

____

____

____

____

____

Actionable Item: Copy and paste the following onto your calendar!

Subject: Be Busy Being Born: Continuous Learning

Time Frame: 15 minutes

Notes: List out the top five books/audiobooks/podcasts that you've been "meaning" to read or listen to. Pull out or download one of these five today!

Next Steps: Calendar 15 minutes every day this week to read/listen to your chosen publication.

Module 2: Your Customer Comes First

introduction

Your Customer at the Center

Customer service is the apex of everything we do. I've been in this business for a long time—as both a practitioner and a consultant. I had an agency for more than thirty years, so I know what it's like to be in the trench. I've been to conferences, meetings, and have even led national program rollouts. Often, at these gatherings, people stand up and recite the catchy slogan, "The customer is the center of everything we do." But that's all it was for many years—a slogan. Not so anymore. The customer truly is in control. What does this mean? The customer decides when they want to buy, how they want to buy, and what they want to buy. That's the environment we're living in today.

Now, don't get me wrong: this doesn't mean we're going to be put out of business. No matter where you're working—in an agency, for a firm, or with a carrier—you need to focus everything you do on the customer. How does each transaction, each presentation, each element of service, affect your customer? This has to be at the forefront of your mind at all times.

The customer decides when they want to buy, how they want to buy, and what they want to buy. That's the environment we're living in today.

Have the mindset that says, "We are going to give such great service that we earn the right to put more products and services into every household and business that we serve." When you adopt this philosophy, you'll find customer coming to you, instead of you having to pursue them!

The customer decides when they want to buy, how they want to buy, and what they want to buy. That's the environment we're living in today.

The opportunity has never been greater. However, we're going to focus on customer service—without regard to commission and revenue. The customer is first. Period. When we do this, the revenue and commissions will come. Give people a reason to do business with you that isn't the rate or the price—and make that reason service—*unrivaled service!*

Practical Application: Create a Perception of Service

Service is perception; you have the ability to make or break this perception. When your customer calls with a question or issue, have effective processes in place. Prescribe a follow-up for each service, to make sure your clients are satisfied every time. This follow-up service contributes to their perception and, ultimately, their reality.

Don't ever simply say, "I'll get back to you." Set a specific time and expectation for your next contact with that customer. Every follow-up, and every call back, should be a scheduled appointment on your calendar. This communicates that their issue is just as important to you as it is to them. When you set specific expectations, you'll be sure to plant the perception of "they come first" into the minds of your clients.

Takeaway Questions:

1. Besides calling or walking into your office, what other ways do customers have access to do business with you (i.e. website, downloadable agency/firm app, etc.)?

____

____

____

____

____

2. Are you consistent with your promise of calling your customers back? Look at your calendar today. For whom can you schedule an appointment that has been waiting for your call?

____

____

____

____

____

Actionable Item: Copy and paste the following onto your calendar!

Subject: Your Customer at the Center: Thank Your Customers

Time Frame: 15 minutes

Notes: Start a list of the last twenty customers who came into, or called into your office in the last week.

Next Steps: Begin assigning five names a day to yourself, and to each team member, to call and thank your clients for their business.

session 1

Four Segments of Clientele

Let's talk for a moment about the customer. Remember, there are only twenty-four hours in a day. I like the saying that goes, "Don't try to get through the day; try to get from the day." To get from the day, you need to be dealing with the right people under the right conditions. There are four different segments of clientele. Let's examine each of these four segments and discern which ones we should be spending the most time on.

The first segment is the **Discussion Partner.** These are clients who don't want to be sold or told; they want a partner to help them make decisions. This is the fastest-growing segment, as well as the most profitable one.

The second segment is the **Relationship Customer.** These clients helped me build my business—and they probably helped you build yours, as well. If you're a carrier or field leader, you grew up in this environment: people buy from people they know and trust. We go to church, synagogue, or mosque with these people; we're in a club with them; our kids know each other; it doesn't matter how you know them—they hand us everything and ask us to handle it all for them.

We all built a living—maybe even a firm—based on relationships. This is the biggest segment in your book, no matter where you work. Odds are these folks came to you because they know and trust you. They're of great value because, with the right nurturing, they'll move up into segment number one and become Discussion Partner clients.

We all built a living—maybe even a firm—based on relationships.

The third segment is the one to be concerned about—everything has changed. These are the **children of those we do business with today (The Generational Client)**. No matter the type of client their parents are, these children comprise their own unique segment. They used to come to us automatically. These clients would say things like, "My daddy was with Troy; his daddy was with Troy; and his daddy's daddy was with Troy. We're going with Troy."

Somewhere around ten years ago, this demographic started to drift away from us. That natural market of growth we used to enjoy begun to dissipate. However, the astute learner—the person who knows this segment well—will get to know the kids *before* you inherit their business. It's important that we think about these folks; our communities don't operate and communicate in the same cozy, hometown way we used to. So, it's up to you to get to know the kids and start a relationship with them early on.

The fourth segment is comprised of **Price People**—that's all they care about. They'll switch every few months to get a better price. And here's the good news: they're not our market. These people belong to the transactional sellers; there are programs out there for them. It's not up to us to cater to their tastes; in fact, it's our responsibility to decide how our time is best spent (with the other three segments). Decide how much time you want to spend with each type of client; but devote the bulk of your time to your Discussion Partner clients.

Practical Application: Grade, or Segment, Your Customers

Both coming in and going out, grade your customers—place them into one of these segments, so you know where to spend the right amount of time. Are they a Discussion Partner? A lead developed by forming a relationship? The children of those you know? Or a transactional client? Once you know where they fall, you can categorize your clientele and decide how much time and marketing funds you want to spend on each group, respectively.

Takeaway Questions:

1. Out of these four groups, which one makes up the most of your current client database?

____

____

____

____

____

2. Which of these four groups do you want to focus on and develop more clients in this year?

____

____

____

____

____

3. What is your strategy to execute developing more of your desired client base?

____

____

____

____

____

Actionable Item: Copy and paste the following onto your calendar!

Subject: Four Segments of Clientele: Segmenting Current Book of Business

Time Frame: 15 minutes

Notes: Pull an electronic report of your entire book of business; including any/all brokered or expertise partnered business.

Next Steps: Begin segmenting and cataloguing results in customers' files.

session 2

What's Your Zone?

What are the guidelines of selecting the right customer in the right segment? I want you to think about how you use the twenty-four hours that you have in a day. How do your team members use their time in the office? I like to say that your biggest expense in the field is your people, although this is also true for carrier offices. Between payroll, benefits, systems and structures, technology and tools, and all the other things you need to make them successful, it truly adds up.

As we think about talking to the right customer under the right conditions, we really need to do a proper assessment. There's a lot changing; but the fundamentals still remain the same. Knowing your zone is one of the most important things you can bring to your organization.

I need to do business the most effective way I can, and that means within a specific radius. Today, I can contact anyone in the world relatively easily: people in Hong Kong, New York, Greece...the list goes on. But does that mean it's wise for me to have a business relationship with clients all around the world? Not necessarily. I don't discount those outside my zone altogether; but I have a different plan for those people than my plan for local clients.

I need to do business the most effective way I can, and that means within a specific radius.

My zone is comprised of a 60-mile radius from where I'm doing business—that's where the bulk of my clients are. I need to do business the most effective way I can, and that means within a specific radius. This way, they can come to me, or I can come to them. Do an assessment of where you're going to market to get to know people—not just market to sell.

Getting to know people requires building a connection with some depth. I can't do that if I'm in California and all of my business is in New York. If you want a surefire way to be most profitable, create a business radius that you adhere to for most of your clients. As you drive down the street, you'll pass by people and businesses that you don't know. Your job is to get to know everybody that you can.

Practical Application: Staying within your Zone

Once you have defined your zone, go about making your name, face and business top-of-mind to everyone within this geographical area. When people think of insurance, you want them to immediately think of your business. Saturate your zone with marketing campaigns, charity events, social mixers, and the like. The more your name and brand can be seen within your community (and the outlying zone areas in your community) the better. Think out of the box. Involve yourself in community events that your competition is not even thinking about.

Takeaway Questions:

1. What's your current radius? Within what parameters do you do business most effectively? Does your current radius need to be adjusted?

____

____

____

____

____

2. What are you doing to foster ongoing communication with clients who don't fall within your radius?

____

____

____

____

____

Actionable Item: Copy and paste the following onto your calendar!

Subject: What's Your Zone? Determining Preferred Business Radius

Time Frame: 15 minutes

Notes: Define a list of all your clients who fall outside of your preferred radius.

Next Steps: Begin creating marketing and communication strategies that pertain only to these clients.

session 3

Transform Your Service Capabilities

A lot of times, I'll go out and do a session with executives, field agents, and firms. Every time I do, I give them a lot of information. Even so, without fail, people still ask me, "What do I do next?"

My answer is, "Transform your service capabilities."

For so many years, our industry has revolved around quoting. Somewhere along the way, we forgot that it's great service that earns the right to put products and services into a customer's household in the first place!

Stop everything, sit down, and decide how *your* organization needs to improve its service capabilities. Do an assessment. What kind of staff do you have? What type of service are they giving? What kinds of tools do you have with which to give great service? Somewhere along the way, we forgot that it's great service that earns the right to put products and services into a customer's household in the first place!

Technology is changing everything, but it will never replace people. It's meant to enhance the service that we give. In the end, it's all about the people.

Somewhere along the way, we forgot that it's great service that earns the right to put products and services into a customer's household in the first place!

Once you've figured out where you need to hire, what systems and processes you need to put in place, and other similar details, you'll begin to see transformation and growth in your organization.

Practical Application: Script Everything

A friend of mine used to say, "Ad libs are for amateurs. All pros practice." I agree—all pros use scripts.

You need a script for all inbound calls, for all outbound calls, for presentations, for follow-up calls, and for every interaction you have with your customers. Sit down and assess the scripts you already have. Once you've done that, you can start, or continue, to create new continuity books.

When everyone's singing from the same songbook, you'll maximize the quality of customer service you provide.

Takeaway Questions:

1. Focus on one aspect of your customer service: it could be phone scripts, presentations, or transactions. How does your procedure for this element affect and serve your customer? What can be improved or changed about this procedure?

____

____

____

____

____

2. Are you utilizing your calendar for all client follow-ups, appointments, drip marketing campaigns, etc.? If not, what's one practical step you can take this week to move towards this habit?

____

____

____

____

____

Actionable Item: Copy and paste the following onto your calendar!

Subject: Transform Your Service Capabilities: Creating Scripts

Time Frame: 15 minutes

Notes: Email support@korsgaden.com for a complimentary copy of their script library templates.

Next Steps: Begin personalizing your templates to best fit your firm's needs.

session 4

Quantum Leaps in Technology

Consistently, whether in person or on social media, I get asked this question in some form: "Are we going to be replaced with technology?"

Allow me to say this: you and I are part of a distribution ecosystem. Technology plays a bigger role than ever in distributing the products and services in this industry; but we're never going to completely be replaced by it. It's not there to replace us. Rather, it's there to enhance the services we provide. People will always want the human touch, but they also want accurate, fast data in this Information Age.

We're still needed, but we would be remiss not to take advantage of the potential that technology offers us to improve our customer service.

Have you ever Googled something and gotten several million results? It's overwhelming. This is how your customers feel when they search for information about insurance and financial services. It's our job to give our customers the content, the information, that's relevant to them. We want to remove the noise and the clutter from the process for them. People will always want the human touch, but they also want accurate, fast data in this Information Age.

People will always want the human touch, but they also want accurate, fast data in this Information Age.

When it comes down to it, people will always need a Discussion Partner to help them navigate the industry, their options, and the right decisions to make for them. That's your role—not to sell, or to tell, but to partner with them! You have the opportunity to impact people's lives—not only today, but for generations in the future. Technology equips you to do this more efficiently and intuitively than ever before. Don't be afraid of technology. Don't be afraid of it taking your business or your job. Think of technology as your friend. Invite it in, but make sure you're using it in such a way that it benefits your customer. Put the customer first.

Practical Application: Assess Your Technology

Someday soon, we'll probably be using holograms to talk to our customers. We can already give presentations virtually, edit and sign documents remotely, and many other amazing things. It's essential to know what we're working with now, and what's on the horizon.

Do an assessment of what you have, and only then look at what you need. When you know what you have, you can better anticipate future needs. What needs to be upgraded? What needs to be introduced for the first time? Have fun with it!

Takeaway Questions:

1. How are you utilizing technology with your personal touch (i.e. social media presence, automated claims, etc.)?

____

____

____

____

____

2. List three elements of your technology that can be immediately implemented to move towards a Discussion Partner model.

____

____

DISCUSSION PARTNER

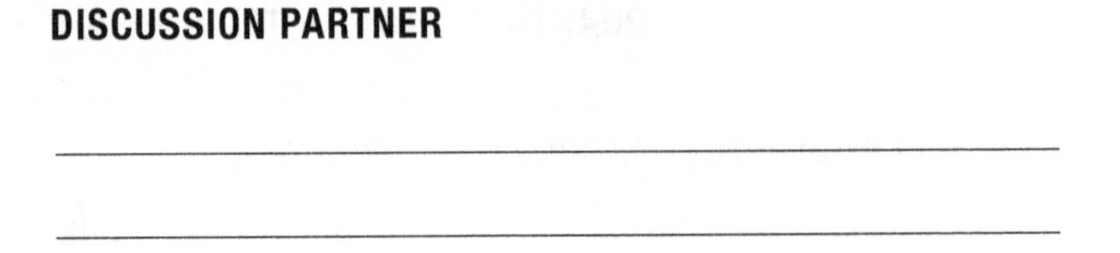

Actionable Item: Copy and paste the following onto your calendar!

Subject: Quantum Leaps in Technology: Social Media Presence

Time Frame: 15 minutes

Notes: Update and strengthen all social media bios, company info, and other information. Determine if any additional social media accounts would benefit your firm.

Next Steps: Calendar a consistent social media "posting" schedule.

session 5

The One with the Most Information Wins

The ability to add more products and services into every household that you serve is earned by assessing what you have at your current disposal. No matter how long we've been in this business, all of us have had this thought at one time or another: "If I could just get John Doe's policies, I could do a lot! If I could get Jane Doe's policies, I could change the world!"

When you're new, it's a lot easier than you think: it's all about relationships—meeting new people, getting to know them, giving presentations, and bringing in new revenue.

We all tend to want what another person has. Instead, let's switch our focus to the customer—earning that right to add more products and services. We need to have a program to deepen our relationships from the moment we meet the customer through the time we have that life cycle of their personal and business insurance needs—that could last decades!

Relationships change everything. That's why computers won't ever replace us—because it's the human touch that makes the difference in this industry. Computers don't know when you're having family problems, when a baby is about to be born. There are a lot of things we know in our relationships with each client that bring great value to them.

We need to have a program to deepen our relationships from the moment we meet the customer through the time we have that life cycle of their personal and business insurance needs—that could last decades!

No matter your position within the organization, think about your relationship with the customer and how you can deepen it every time you talk with them.

Practical Application: Get More Information

How do you deepen relationships? Get more contact information and reasons to call. Get his email; her email; the kids' emails; their social media handles; you want it all. The one with the most information wins. Have a repeatable system to gather more information each time you touch your client.

Takeaway Questions:

1. Do you have a systematic way of collecting data every time you interact with a client? If not, create a plan to implement one. If you do, does it need to be updated/revamped?

____

____

____

____

____

2. How consistent are you and your team in collecting information from clients? What is one immediate change you can make to strengthen this consistency?

____

____

____

____

____

3. Are you utilizing technology to enhance your service to your customers? If not, what do you think is holding you back?

____

DISCUSSION PARTNER

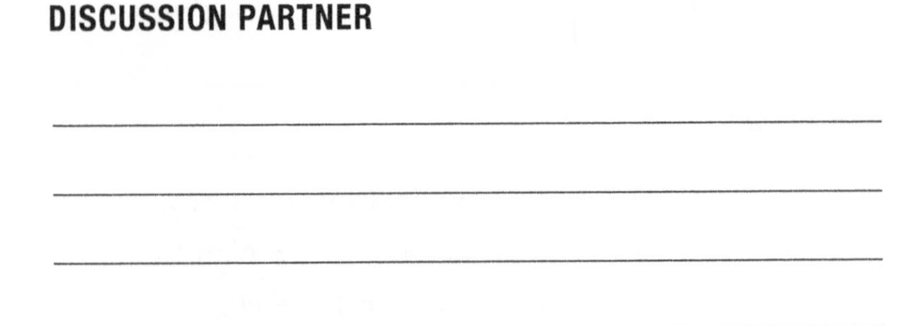

Actionable Item: Copy and paste the following onto your calendar!

Subject: The One with the Most Information Wins: Create a Data Sheet to Capture Customer Information

Time Frame: 15 minutes

Notes: Email support@korsgaden.com for a complimentary copy of their data sheet template.

Next Steps: Customize your template and create a consistent strategy to use within your firm.

session 6

A Product Spectrum

One of the things we suggest is that you're organized and efficient. One way to ensure organization is to make sure you have all the right scripts; in addition, let's introduce having the right workflows and questionnaires. The way you talk to people is important. How prompt you are when you gather information is also important.

You don't want people to come in and feel like they've got to spend the entire day with you. In a perfect world, we would all go paperless. But the reality is that some clients still like to touch and see a "hard" copy. For that reason, you want to color-code everything. Auto might be one color; home might be another; business insurance is another; life insurance is another. You want to have a product spectrum: one sheet with all the products and services you offer. You'll use that sheet with your client as you move forward, to let them know that you offer advice on everything for which you have a license.

We need to be compliant with the Department of Insurance, and we need to make sure that we're lock-step with our carriers' compliance rules, as well. It's easy to put these worksheets together. Every desk should be set up the same way in your operation—with access to all the right forms. If I'm licensed, I can grab the form and ask the questions to every customer I talk to that day.

You may have a 360-degree view on your client's household or business; but every time you talk to them, you should always be looking for new information.

You may have a 360-degree view on your client's household or business; but every time you talk to them, you should always be looking for new information. These sheets help you to know whether they have the same job, have a new 401k plan at work, have started a new business, and other important details. If you want to use these in an electronic form, all the better. Regardless, set up a system—a repeatable process—to make it easier on yourself, your team, and your clients.

Practical Application: Product Spectrum

I like to have a blank printed product spectrum available every time I have a face-to-face meeting with a client. As I wrap up the appointment, I'll pull out the spectrum and say, "Somewhere on this page are services you've always wanted to know more about. Would you take a few seconds and circle the ones that interest you?" Most people circle one or two. Others will circle half a page. Some will circle nothing—and that's okay. I use this information to set up "touch points" throughout the year. Now, I am contacting my customer based on their requests and interests, not mine.

Takeaway Questions:

1. Do you currently have and/or use a product spectrum or similar form in your firm?

____

____

____

____

____

2. How can you improve your current follow-up process in order to glean new information from clients each time you talk to them (i.e. utilizing CRM to determine needed/missing info)?

DISCUSSION PARTNER

____

____

____

____

____

3. Do you and your team know all of the products and services offered through the carriers/companies you represent?

____

____

____

____

____

Actionable Item: Copy and paste the following onto your calendar!

Subject: Product Spectrum: Creating a Product Spectrum

Time Frame: 15 minutes

Notes: Email support@korsgaden.com for a complimentary copy of their Product Spectrum template.

Next Steps: Customize the template based on all products and services your firm has access to through the carries/companies you represent.

session 7

Concierge Service

What does it mean to make concierge service the standard? I've been writing, talking about, and helping implement concierge service in carriers, firms, brokers, and agencies for years. This system is effective because it makes you stand out.

Here's how it works: you create a position in your organization where somebody is accountable for calling customers back to ensure their satisfaction with the service, they received from you. Do this within 24 hours of the customer's original contact for maximum effectiveness; and again, make sure to script everything to ensure consistency.

This is important because you'll hear some positive feedback. When your concierge calls, many customers will say something like, "Oh, I was very happy with the service I received from Jane. She's awesome." We can go back to Jane now and give her affirmation and encouragement. The next time she handles an issue, she'll still be giving great service.

Create a position in your organization where somebody is accountable for calling customers back to ensure their satisfaction with the service, they received from you.

Not everybody will always be happy. Within 24 hours, you'll know about the issue. Now, you can work together to give that customer the kind of service that they desire and have every right to expect. You won't be trying to do damage control a month, three months, or a year too late. You're on top of any issue with this immediate follow-up strategy.

Create a position in your organization where somebody is accountable for calling customers back to ensure their satisfaction with the service, they received from you.

For those folks who are happy, we have a chance to pivot and offer more products and services. Remember, put the customer first in every interaction. Feel out their satisfaction and use that as a determining factor for how to conduct further interactions and business with them.

Practical Application: Block Time

Blocking time is essential for offering concierge service. No matter your role or rank, you'll probably end up making these calls on occasion. Create a position if you can—it's a goldmine. No matter who does it, make sure that person sets aside time to make these calls.

Blocking time may seem to take away from your other responsibilities and revenue; in reality, it multiplies it: retention goes up, customer satisfaction goes up, and revenue goes up!

Takeaway Questions:

1. Who could you immediately assign concierge duties to in your office? What practical steps can you take towards this in the next month?

____

____

____

____

____

2. What is your current procedure for handling dissatisfied customers? Is everyone on your team fully aware of this strategy? Do you roleplay scenarios with your team on how to best handle these types of situations?

____

____

____

____

____

Actionable Item: Copy and paste the following onto your calendar!

Subject: Concierge Service: Integrating Concierge Service

Time Frame: 15 minutes

Notes: Email support@korsgaden.com for complimentary copies of Concierge Job Description and Concierge Script templates.

Next Steps: Assign the Concierge position to an existing team member or begin recruiting for a new team member to fill this position.

Module 3: Expertise Partners

introduction

Why Does Specialization Matter?

Where does specialization fit into the Discussion Partner program? Specialization is essential—it's the foundation of being able to grow your operation. When I started out, I was given a big book of business called the phone book. I dialed for dollars. I was everything to as many people as I could reach. Then, when I hired my first employee, they became a mini-me: a generalist who did a little of everything.

Eventually, I realized that recreating myself wasn't the answer. Instead, I developed a team of high-performance specialists who each focused on one area of products and services. I hired someone to help me in auto—they became a profit center; I had somebody come on to help me with life—they became a profit center. Someone else came on to help me with property...you get the idea. I realized that recreating myself wasn't the answer. Instead, I developed a team of high-performance specialists who each focused on one area of products and services.

I realized that recreating myself wasn't the answer. Instead, I developed a team of high-performance specialists who each focused on one area of products and services.

Finally, I replaced myself altogether. If I didn't want to be in the agency, I didn't have to be. There are people who have taken specialization to a whole new level: they've created firms with twenty, fifty, or a hundred people. Distribution organizations can number into the thousands. Specialization has grown from being an expert in one field to having expertise positions even when they're not on your payroll.

As we think about expertise partners, it doesn't always have to be a service or product line that you yourself take on. Think about aviation, marine, excess insurance, or high-end financial services—you can't be all things to all people. That's okay because, with expertise partners, you can *still* be the gateway your clients need to the right products and services for them.

You may not make as much "up front" commission; but by giving the client the information they need; you'll grow your business and your partnerships every day.

Takeaway Questions:

1. Have you tried to "recreate" yourself, or to hire more generalists? How has this worked out for you? If you have, did you experience difficulties with training (i.e. where to start, finding time, comprehension and retainment, etc.)?

____

____

____

____

____

2. What's one area of expertise that you aren't well-versed in? What is the one area of your business that you least enjoy doing?

____

____

____

____

____

Actionable Item: Copy and paste the following onto your calendar!

Subject: Why Does Specialization Matter: Replacing Myself

Time Frame: 15 minutes

Notes: Determine what area(s) to begin replacing yourself first in.

Next Step: Start to catalogue your procedures of these areas to create job descriptions and continuity books for your new hire(s).

session 1

Why Specialization Works

Why does specialization work? There are two types of agencies: a generalist agency and a specialist agency. A generalist agency is how most people get into the business. They know a little bit about everything, but they don't know enough to really offer the client what they need all the time. They need expertise advice.

Earlier, I mentioned that when I started out in the business, I was the "king of everything"—auto, life, property, business...the problem with this model is that I was just running in circles. I see this all the time when visiting field offices. I'll go into an office and ask leaders, "How's this employee doing for you?" They'll answer, "She's fine. She's really busy. She's doing a great job—she's so busy."

As a specialist, you're an expert at one thing. We can measure and monitor your success. I ask, "Well, is Jane truly helping the customer? Is she helping your bottom line?" They're not so sure about those answers. When I tell crowds this story, they usually laugh, because they can relate to it. You can't go through your day running around, trying to be all things to all people. It's not profitable, it's frustrating, and it doesn't help your client.

As a specialist, you're an expert at one thing. We can measure and monitor your success.

Why does specialization work? Because, as a specialist, you're an expert at one thing. We can measure and monitor your success. We can tell if you're a profit center, because we're not measuring you by how much you run all over the place, but rather by how effectively you serve clients.

Working together as a team of specialists—expertise partners—we create a high-performance team. It works because it's all in concert to help the client.

Practical Application: Generalist or Specialist?

You've got to decide which kind of agency you are. Draw a line in the sand. The next person that you hire must be a specialist. It'll be difficult, but you can make the transition. Explain to your team that having a specialist takes things off of their plate. Their lives—and yours—become easier, now that this specialist is the resident expert in that area! If you're not currently in a position to hire, start converting existing staff. This is easier than you think! Your staff is already naturally gravitating toward the areas they are best at and prefer to do. Set up true boundaries – swim lanes – with which to move toward the Specialist Model.

Takeaway Questions:

1. Based on your current team structure, do you find it easy to measure and monitor your team's profitability? Why or why not?

____

____

____

____

____

2. Ask your team for honest feedback. In what areas do they already feel they are "experts"? What areas do they enjoy the most? What areas do they least enjoy?

____

____

____

____

____

____

3.What area(s) of the firm would benefit from an Expertise Partner relationship?

____

____

____

____

____

Actionable Item: Copy and paste the following onto your calendar!

Subject: Why Specialization Works: Moving Toward a Specialist Firm

Time Frame: 15 minutes

Notes: What immediate changes can be made to reposition your current team members to a Specialist Model?

Next Steps: Have your team members begin cataloging processes and procedures to create job descriptions and continuity books for your new hire(s).

session 2

Creating an Organizational Chart

The first thing we need to do in specialization is create an organizational chart. It seems easy; but you need to figure out what the workflows are in your agency, firm, or carrier operation. This chart helps you define what services and products you're giving to your customers—and who's accountable for that information.

You're always growing, but we want to grow by putting on more productive capacity—more team members. We've got to integrate these team members under the right conditions. By creating an organizational chart, we define what's needed for the organization without regard to who's in it today. Every box starts out blank. Then, we begin to fill them in.

Sometimes, because we're a generalist operation—either at the carrier level or at the street level—we'll have three, five, or ten people in the same box. In that case, you can create more boxes around it. But the key here is figuring out which person will be accountable for which responsibilities.

Create your organizational chart with a clean slate. Don't look back; look at where you are today, and where you want to be in the future.

Create your organizational chart with a clean slate. Don't look back; look at where you're at today, and where you want to be in the future. Decide your priorities, and how they will be executed as you move forward.

You can see this all beginning to tie together—we need scripts; we need continuity books; we need job descriptions; we need accountability service statements for everybody in the organization—from the CEO to those who are team members out in the field. We're all in this to serve the customer.

Practical Application: Look at Other Industries

As you form your organizational chart, don't look merely at how those in our industry are doing it—look at other industries. Some of the greatest positions we've created and helped implement have been inspired by other industries.

A dentist, a retailer, a call center—it doesn't matter where you look: you'll find principles and practices that help you form your chart. "Be open to all things, and attached to nothing," as the Stoic philosophy says.

Takeaway Questions:

1. Do you currently have an organization chart for your firm? If so, when was the last time you updated or amended it?

____

____

____

____

____

2. What is one other industry you can look to for inspiration and assistance as you update your organizational workflow?

____

____

____

____

____

3. If you could reorganize your entire team today (including yourself), what would that look like? What does it look like in five years from today? Ten years?

____

____

____

____

____

Actionable Item: Copy and paste the following onto your calendar!

Subject: Creating an Organizational Chart: Reorganizing for the Future

Time Frame: 15 minutes

Notes: Create a Specialist Model org chart based on your current team members. Give each team member a blank org chart and ask them to do the same.

Next Steps: Compile all org charts and notes to determine long-term structure, next hire needs, and current team transitioning strategies.

session 3

Selecting Your First Specialty

Which specialist position should come first? I still get this question every time I speak to a boardroom or large audience. I used to say, "Whichever position you feel the most behind in, so that you can relieve that pressure and get everybody on the offense." With that being said, I've since changed my mind.

Now, I advise that you ask yourself, "What does the customer need the most?" It could be auto, if that's what matters most to your consumers. This isn't about margins and profits, primarily; it's about serving your clients' needs. The customer could need products and services in an area in which you don't have expertise; if it's a worthwhile investment, you can bring in an expertise partner to help you develop that department in your organization.

The first person you hire is the one that the client needs the most. Regardless of how you do it, or how much profit it brings you, here's the bottom line: The first person you hire is the one that the client needs the most! When that area and team member becomes a profit center, you add the next specialist, and the next, and the next...never stop growing.

Practical Application: Have an Onboarding System

If you're planning on onboarding an expertise partner who's not on your payroll, you've got to have a process to bring them into your organization. Onboarding is crucial—someone is becoming part of your bigger picture—they're joining your entire team.

The first person you hire is the one that the client needs the most.

Have an onboarding schedule, including orientation, introductions, and everything critical to their success. It all comes together; so, help them understand that every team member affects their job; and, likewise, they affect everyone else, as well. Make this system intuitive, and you'll be setting up your team as a whole for success. Consistency is key.

Takeaway Questions:

1. Do you have a consistent and comprehensive onboarding process? What areas can be improved upon, added to, or completely removed from your current process?

____

____

____

____

____

2. Looking at your customer base and your current team, what's the first specialist you want to add to your organization?

____

____

____

____

____

Actionable Item: Copy and paste the following onto your calendar!

Subject: Selecting Your First Specialty: Who to Hire Next

DISCUSSION PARTNER

Time Frame: 15 minutes

Notes: What is the one major area of your firm are your clients being underserved in? How could a designated Specialist fill the gaps?

Next Steps: Begin customizing a job description for the position you are looking to fill. Define the role BEFORE you find the person to fill the position.

session 4

Hiring Profit Centers

We keep coming back to the idea that you need a roadmap. You need a master plan. Knowing who the customer needs the most, how to execute that onboarding, and how your future is laid out in terms of a timeline are all essential.

In the old days, I used to say that every person had six months to be a profit center. Now, I think most of us know in our gut if they're a profit center within the first thirty days. If I walk by their office and the person's staring at a blank screen, odds are they're not going to be a profit center; or the person that onboarded them didn't show them how to flip the screen on. You just have a sense about when somebody's going to fit into your team.

When we hire people, we suggest looking for two qualities: a good attitude and a desire to grow. As you go about enacting your strategy, the first step is hiring the right person. The next part is having a roadmap for this staff member specifically, and a prioritization that allows them to understand what's expected of them. When you do this, your new hire can exceed your expectations, because they know what you're looking for in their role.

When we hire people, we suggest looking for two qualities: a good attitude and a desire to grow.

Practical Application: Don't Wait Twelve Months

Don't wait a year to decide whether or not your new hire has become a profit center. Everything today is about speed and consistency. When you're hiring somebody, speed to profit is important. We can't wake up twelve months from now and say, "Oh, that person didn't work out."

If I'm paying somebody, $3,000 per month over the course of a year...that adds up. For every action, there's an equal and opposite reaction. You must inspect what you expect and ensure that your new hires are profit centers.

Takeaway Questions:

1. Do you have a systematic process in place to consistently evaluate your team, including your new hires?

____

____

___

___

___

2. Do you currently have a roadmap for your team members that defines your expectations for them? Do you currently communicate to your team desired benchmarks and Key Performance Indicators (KPIs)? Does your team understand what is required of them to be "successful" in your eyes? What are those indicators?

___

___

___

___

___

Actionable Item: Copy and paste the following onto your calendar!

Subject: Hiring Profit Centers: Creating a Consistent Evaluation Process

Time Frame: 15 minutes

Notes: Begin creating benchmarks and expectations for current team members, as well as potential future new hires.

Next Steps: Consistently meet with your team (in groups and one-on-one) to reiterate these benchmarks and expectations. Use these meetings to help mentor and guide your team to success.

This will be especially important when it comes to new hires. You will want to continuously monitor their progress over the first ninety days to determine if they are a Profit Center or a Cost Center.

session 5

Communication is Crucial

Communication: it's one of the most important pieces in executing specialization. Communication is everything. Why? Because, if you're in a large organization, you need the message to be consistent; in a smaller organization, it can make the difference between immediate profit and immediate loss.

How we communicate to our team members—and, more importantly, our clients—is essential. Our customers need to know that we're transitioning into more of a customer-service-oriented organization. How we state this has to be concise and simple. You've probably heard the phrase "elevator pitch." It's a point of contact where you get your message to a person. It doesn't take a lot of time or money.

Billions of dollars are spent on advertising; but I submit to you that talking directly to a consumer is the best advertising. In a very short period of time—a minute or two—you can get across what you're trying to accomplish. In specialization, the message is this: "To better serve you, we are creating expertise partners within our organization. We can't be all things to all people; yet we want to offer you the kind of service you desire and have every right to expect. For that reason, we're hiring more people, and creating more relationships with people to give you the advice that's important to you."

Billions of dollars are spent on advertising; but I submit to you that talking directly to a consumer is the best advertising.

Practical Application: Get Everyone in the Room

Get the entire team in the room. Whether you have two people or two thousand, get them all in the same place. Figure out what you're trying to communicate. You may break into smaller groups at some point; but make sure you're all singing off the same song sheet.

Everyone has to believe in what you're doing. Create a culture that is service-oriented at its core. To do this, you need a strong foundation—unity. If I want to have a good specialization program, I need to sit down and say, "How does this affect my customer?" Get your team's feedback and come up with your core statement.

Takeaway Questions:

1. When is the best time to get your entire team together for this vision-casting meeting? Choose a day and time that can be replicated every week, every other week, or monthly, based on your needs (i.e. the second Tuesday of every month at 10:00am).

____

____

____

____

____

2. Before you meet, create an agenda. Keep your meetings brief and on point. Discuss both global changes and initiatives, as well as local and personalized ones. Allow your team to weigh in and collaborate on solutions and integration.

____

____

____

____

____

Actionable Item: Copy and paste the following onto your calendar!

Subject: Communication is Crucial: Setting Staff Meetings

Time Frame: 15 minutes

Notes: Immediately schedule a staff meeting. Keep this brief—about 30 minutes or less. Begin defining your agenda for this meeting.

Next Steps: Determine if the date and time worked for your last staff meeting. Schedule ongoing meetings on consistent times and days. Put reminders on your calendar to prepare an agenda in advance.

session 6

Making the Change

How do we make the change and continue the transformation?

It's not as easy as one might think. I've watched a lot of agencies—especially exclusive, but also independent—struggle with adding productive capacity and specialization. Why? Because they've been doing the same thing for so many years. They start and stop transformation, defaulting back to their old way of doing business.

Decide what you'll do to have a journey of transformation, knowing that certain forces will try to derail you. That's why communication with your current staff and customers is so important—it becomes a way of life. Constantly be asking yourself, "Is this change affecting the customer in the right way? Is this the right person for this position?"

Look at what you're doing, and retool your agency, firm, or carrier operation. Nothing is going to stay the same in our business. There's a tsunami of change coming today, and that's why you must become a Discussion Partner Operation. Once you do, you need to keep moving to stay ahead of the wave of change.

Transformation is constant.

There's a tsunami of change coming today, and that's why you must become a Discussion Partner operation.

Practical Application: Know Where You Are

To put specialization into place in your agency, you need to know where you are today. Segment your organization and distribution to find the best solutions for you. My hiring issues at the start were different from the ones I had when I serviced thousands of clients.

You want to assess your operation, go to organizations that are similar in size and scope, and look at what they're doing. Only when you know where you are can you transform effectively.

Takeaway Questions:

1. Identify one organization similar in size and scope to yourself that you can look to for inspiration and motivation. What are they doing well?

____

____

____

____

____

2. As you transition and change, what are some of the "forces" that may try to derail you? What challenges can you anticipate for your organization (i.e. pushback from current team members, lack of immediate funds, etc.)?

____

____

____

____

____

____

Actionable Item: Copy and paste the following onto your calendar!

Subject: Making the Change: Identify Growth Opportunities

Time Frame: 15 minutes

Notes: List out 3–5 things your firm does exceptionally well. What makes these so exceptional in your point of view?

Next Steps: How can you build upon these foundations, or apply them to other areas of your business?

Module 4: Power Position

introduction

The Purpose of Power Positioning

One of my books, *Power Position Your Agency,* is still a best-seller in the insurance industry. It amazes me how many people will come up to me during one of my live presentations and say, "I read your book, and it changed the way I did business." Although it has been in publication for over two decades, there have only been a few minor updates. The fundamentals discussed in the book have, and will, continue to stand the test of time.

Some of the processes are not as relevant today as they once were; but I would be remiss if I didn't talk about some of the foundational success you can have by power positioning your agency.

My success over the years can be directly linked to the foundations that I laid out for my business early in my career.

Throughout the years, I would adapt and change as dictated by the industry. However, I never wavered from the basic tenets that defined my operation.

I would be remiss if I didn't talk about some of the foundational success you can have by power positioning your agency.

In this module, we'll explore what power positioning is, how you can go about doing it, and the affects it will have on you, your team, your organization, and your industry.

Takeaway Questions:

1. Older systems and structures from past years are mentioned in the introduction. In your experience, what systems in the insurance and financial services industry have become out-of-date or ineffective?

____

____

____

____

____

2. Of those, which ones are you still using in your operation today? Which ones are part of your carrier/company's

proprietary legacy system? If they can't be replaced, how can you either work around them or utilize them more effectively?

____

____

____

____

____

Actionable Item: Copy and paste the following onto your calendar!

Subject: The Purpose of Power Positioning: Defining Outdated Processes and Systems

Time Frame: 15 minutes

Notes: Review all your current processes. Define any that are out of date, cumbersome, or redundant.

Next Steps: Based on your findings, begin creating a strategy to replace, update, or create work arounds for out-of-date processes and systems.

session 1

The Agency Contact Representative

Probably the most important thing in the book *Power Position Your Agency* is the concept of the Agency Contact Representative. Long ago, I decided that the operation needed somebody to be on the offensive—to make sure that we were having consistent reviews with our clients; to make sure that we were offering products these households and businesses didn't already have; to make sure that we were contacting new prospective clients.

We all wanted to do this; we just didn't have time. Whether your organization has one person or ten people, there needs to be somebody dedicated to making sure people are in front of you and your team all day long. They could take away all the systems that are out there...this is the last system I would let go of: making sure that I'm seeing enough clients under the right conditions.

There needs to be somebody dedicated to making sure people are in front of you and your team all day long.

There's a job description in the book for this; it's improved, though it hasn't changed a lot. This fundamental principle of seeing people under the right conditions for reviews—all the combinations and caveats that encompasses—falls under this one team member's job description. There's nothing else in the operation they need to do.

Years later, people still come up to me and say, "Do I still need an Agency Contact Representative (ACR)?" And I say, "Without a doubt." I could do an entire seminar today just on putting this position into place. Hire the ACR first, before you hire a production assistant. You want to be the most effective you can be, and then have all your production assistants be more productive by having someone to set them appointments under the right conditions.

Practical Application: Create a Job Description

The first thing you need to do is create a job description. If you haven't read Power Position Your Agency, or you don't have access to my job description, get ahold of us at support@korsgaden.com. These have been successfully used in thousands of offices throughout the U.S. and abroad. It costs you nothing; it just takes a little time to email us, and we'll get the job description to you.

Takeaway Questions:

1. Do you currently have someone fulfilling the basic role of the Agency Contact Representative in your organization? If not, what do you think has been holding you back from making that position (i.e. lack of time finding someone, didn't see the need, lack of funds, etc.)?

____

____

____

____

____

2. What's one practical step you can take this week to move towards having an ACR on your team (i.e. define their role, list a job posting on a hiring site, use social media to attract candidates, etc.)?

____

____

____

____

Actionable Item: Copy and paste the following onto your calendar!

Subject: The Agency Contact Representative: Part-Time Employee

Time Frame: 15 minutes

Notes: Email support@korsgaden.com for a complimentary copy of the ACR job description template.

Next Steps: Customize the template to fit the needs of your firm.

session 2

Make Them Come to You

Years ago, when I started implementing and executing *Power Position Your Agency,* I realized that within my own organization—and others we studied—most people resisted having people come into the office. But we studied other industries, and we noticed that, if you give somebody enough reasons, they'll come in. It has to be important to them. The dentist doesn't go out to fix your cavity on your couch; your doctor doesn't come to your home—most of them, anyway. Most retail is done in the store—not over the phone or in a digital experience. People like to touch and feel and see what they're buying and meet the people who are providing them with the service.

This doesn't mean that the ecosystem doesn't involve digital or a call center—it does. But we can't just default to saying that these options are what the customer wants, because they aren't. If you ask your customers if they want to come in, and you give them enough reasons, you'll find that they do.

If you give somebody enough reasons, they'll come in.

Just look at financial services alone: people have hundreds of thousands—even millions—of dollars. They're not going to handle all their business over the phone. Every once in a while, they want to come in to make sure it's real. In addition, all your tools are there: your team, your computers, your files...you can't simply pick all of that up and go do business on somebody's couch. Again, you need to give people enough reasons to come to you. You're going to want to sit down and figure out what those reasons are; but I believe there is value in people coming to you at least once a year. It was true twenty years ago, it's true today, and it will be true in the future.

To be top of mind, you need to constantly be touching your customer through personal interactions, digital communication, advertising, and so on. You want to touch your customers at least seven times a year. You need them to come to you; once they stop coming to you in person, they're either going to start going to somebody else or they're going to go completely digital. You offer personal service; and personal service is done in person.

Practical Application: Roleplay with Your Team

Get everybody to roleplay in the operation—have them practice getting someone to come into the office. It's easier than you think. Roleplay becomes a conditioning for the staff—it gives them confidence. When they have confidence, they almost demand that the customer comes in. The customer *wants* you to tell them to come in. You need to do so and give them the reasons *why*. Roleplay to make this sound like a conversation. With everybody singing from the same song sheet, you'll see people coming through your door all day long.

Takeaway Questions:

1. List the top 3-5 reasons you believe a client should come into your office. Share these with your team.

____

____

____

____

2. Have you ever set up a roleplay with your team to practice inviting clients into the office? When is the soonest you can have a roleplay exercise with your staff?

____

____

____

____

3. On average, how many times per year would you say you're touching each client (either through in-person meetings, digital correspondence, snail mail, phone/web calls, etc.)?

____

____

____

____

Actionable Item: Copy and paste the following onto your calendar!

Subject: Make Them Come to You: Create a Marketing Matrix

Time Frame: 15 minutes

Notes: Email support@korsgaden.com for a complimentary copy of their *7 Touch Marketing Matrix* template.

Next Steps: Customize the template to match your firm's products and services. Begin building a strategy to implement this for every household and business you serve.

session 3

Your Review Program

There are some real cornerstones—some real musts—you need in order to have a successful operation, no matter what size you are. You must have a review program—some way to meet with your clients at least once a year. You want that 360-degree view of them, their family, their business, and the other aspects of their lives. You also want to be sure to use this time to gather all the various methods of contacting them, including new ones. This also includes reasons to call them, and methods of prescribing products and services in order to give them options on what they purchase. You do this by having a planned review every year.

I like to say, "If you give us 15 or 30 minutes one time a year, we'll worry about your insurance program the other 364 days of the year." Now, does that mean you're not going to talk to them throughout the year? No. But by coming in and giving you enough time to get all the information you need, they allow you to give *them* information—on any new programs, about the changing market, and so on. You'll glean information that will allow you to contact them throughout the year under the right conditions.

I like to say, "If you give us 15 or 30 minutes one time a year, we'll worry about your insurance program the other 364 days of the year."

There's always something new to talk about. This is a planned way for you to meet with the decision-maker in the household or business. It's not a selling interview; it's an information-gathering and an information-giving interview. You will then set up a plan to talk to them throughout the year through correspondence, other meetings, video chats—whatever they prefer.

But again—bring them into the office and have the decision-maker be in the room. You don't need everybody from the business; you need the decision-maker. You don't need everybody in the household; you need the decision-maker. Why? They'll go back and tell the others what's needed. You're providing the content—the information; they're providing advice to the rest of the group on what's needed next.

Get them to come into the office and set all the other systems up around that review.

Practical Application: Set a Number of Appointments Per Day

Figure out how many in-office appointments with clients you can handle per day. I like to think that the average person working in the business can handle a minimum of four reviews per day, along with their other prospect-related business. You give service primarily by having that 360-degree view of your clients we talked about—by being a Discussion Partner. Re-sell them on why they're with you and lay out a roadmap for how you're going to touch them throughout the rest of the year.

Takeaway Questions:

1. Do you currently have an annual review process that requires clients to come into the office and meet with your team? What do you need to do to implement, or improve, this process?

____

____

____

____

____

2. How many reviews a day are you conducting? How many of these reviews does your team conduct per day? Do you foresee a need to expand your team to accommodate your clients?

____

____

____

____

____

Actionable Item: Copy and paste the following onto your calendar!

Subject: Your Review Program: Create/Update a Consistent Review Program

Time Frame: 15 minutes

Notes: Email support@korsgaden.com for their Annual Review script templates.

Next Steps: Customize scripts to best fit the needs of your firm. Spend time roleplaying scripts with your current team, including your ACR.

session 4

A Right-to-the-Point Approach

In *Power Position Your Agency,* one of the things I tried to get across was this: be direct and be right to the point. The same is true today. The popular word now is "transparency." I believe in transparency—the same transparency that's available today in financial services is starting to be applied in property and casualty.

I want to be transparent about where I make money and where I don't make money. People know I'm a for-profit business; so, if I own a business, I'm not ashamed to say when I make money. Now, the law doesn't require me to expose every penny; but I also want them to know when I'm making money, and when I'm not.

I make money on the big picture. I don't make money on every transaction. Clients look at that and think, "Wow.

That's honesty. I like that. I'm comfortable with this person, because they're not always trying to sell me something."

I want to be transparent about where I make money and where I don't make money.

Being right to the point is also helpful when it comes to claims situations. When I was in agency—directly affecting the consumer—if they had a claim and it wasn't covered, I would say, "That's not covered, and here's why." Not everything is covered by insurance. There are some common-sense exclusions; and then, there are some common-sense forms in certain areas where things are not covered. People can accept that; they just want to know why.

One of the reasons we believe in being direct is because, when you have the information, you can be more transparent and honest with somebody about what's covered and what's not covered. Learn every day, so you can be direct and be honest with your customers.

Practical Application: Be Direct but not Pushy

Being direct with a client when you are detailing what you're doing for them is great. However, there is a fine line between being direct and being pushy. You never want to make a client feel like you're pressuring or coercing them into buying something they don't feel they need. Always give your clients all the options available to them; but be sure to listen to what they are saying they need—not what *you* think they should buy!

Takeaway Questions:

1. How do you show transparency to your clients about where you make money (and where you don't)? Tactfully explain to your client the things you (and your firm) do that are required, and the things you do that are above and beyond – the value you add to their lives.

____

____

____

____

____

2. Do you and your team explain policy limits and claim details, including what is covered and what is *not* covered, during the initial sell and/or review of a policy? How can you improve this explanation process?

____

____

____

____

____

Actionable Item: Copy and paste the following onto your calendar!

Subject: A Right-to-the-Point Approach: Creating Transparency

Time Frame: 15 minutes

Notes: Define which processes and procedures in your firm are "required" and which are "value added."

Next Steps: Create a script/word tracks for you and your team to tactfully explain these to clients. Create scripts for claims, service transactions, new business, etc.

session 5

Who is Your Market?

In *Power Position Your Agency,* I talk about marketing to your market. Let me bring it into today's world. There are certain types of people that you know are going to fit into the way you do business. They might be doctors, UPS drivers, or medical professionals. They fit a profile in which their propensity to do business with you is greater than others. Choose where you can win the most business. Who needs what you have the most? That way, you start identifying these markets.

Go to them in such a way that they feel as if they're coming to you.

People buy from people they know and trust; plus, people refer other people in their field. Be mindful of this—I learned this lesson from a friend a long time ago: the doctor refers the nurse; the nurse usually doesn't refer the doctor (unless you ask them to do so). So, you've got to cultivate relationships, instead of waiting for them to go to you. Go to them in such a way that they feel as if they're coming to you.

Start working a network of doctors, UPS drivers, or whatever demographic you're going after—people who socialize together. If one will pay more for value, they will sell all the other people on why they should do business with you—even if you may be high-cost in certain areas.

Birds of a feather flock together.

Practical Application: Become an Expert in One Thing

There are certain fundamentals that still work within the new world. One of them is that you need to be an expert in a certain field. I chose transportation when I first got into the business. This was a large, underserved opportunity in my area.

I was an expert in that because I studied it, I got to know the people, and I started a network in which I got natural referrals. Then, I applied the same process in hospitality. Then, in medical...you get the idea. I start with one specialty. Become an expert in the product and become an expert in having relationships in that field.

Takeaway Questions:

1. What field are you an expert in now? What field(s) are you interested in becoming an expert in?

2.What associations or groups are you currently involved in that could provide you with Affinity Group contact lists?

3. Identify places within your current book of business where Affinity Groups could be created. Then, start creating them!

Actionable Item: Copy and paste the following onto your calendar!

Subject: Your Market: Creating Affinity Groups

Time Frame: 15 minutes

Notes: Define 1–3 industries you would like to focus on doing more business within the future.

Next Steps: Start creating lists of prospective clients in these industries and create a marketing plan to implement and execute with those lists.

session 6

Make It Simple

One of the reasons that *Power Position Your Agency* is still popular today is because it's simple. If you make things simple, people will do it. I made the processes simple because I had a short attention span, but it really helped people see how easy things could be.

Make everything simple so it's easy to do.

If we make it too complicated, nobody wants to do it. If our presentation is too complicated, nobody wants to buy in, or do business with you. A lot of us try to look smarter than we really are—we use big words; we don't keep it simple or put it into their terms. Then, they don't end up doing business with us for a number of reasons. Learn to put it into the customer's language.

Simplify the processes in your office—whether it's a review system, a 360-degree view of the customer system...make everything simple so it's easy to do. You want to do this because, if you do, it will become a repeatable process.

Practical Application: Make It Simple

You don't want to have to push your staff—you want them to be pulling you. How do you do this? Make it simple. At many conferences I've gone to, I've returned with inspiration for my office and my team. I'd tell my staff, "We're going to change everything!"

They wouldn't typically like that. Why? It's too complicated. They've got things to do. I began to realize that the one thing we all have in common is we want things to be simple and easy.

Decide what you want to do and sell your team through communicating properly and simply. If the message is important, communicate it at least three times before you begin to execute—that way, it will become their process—not just your process.

Takeaway Questions:

1. What's one practical way you can simplify office procedures for you and your staff (i.e. move toward specialization, create defined job descriptions, eliminate redundancies in office procedures, etc.)?

____

____

____

____

____

2. Think of one practice or system you want to implement in your team. How can you begin communicating about it now, before you execute it, so that the team takes ownership of it alongside you?

____

____

____

____

____

Actionable Item: Copy and paste the following onto your calendar!

Subject: Make it Simple: Streamlining Workflows

Time Frame: 15 minutes

Notes: Identify where most of the bottlenecks occur in your firm's service procedures.

Next Steps: Work with your current team to create and implement streamlined, seamless processes and procedures.

Module 5: Marketing and Lead Development

introduction:

The Importance of Lead Generation

In this section, I want to talk about lead generation. The reason is that it's important. It's also one of the biggest questions I get—at conferences, behind the curtain with carriers, and out in the field. There are so many options, and I want to talk about all of them—what we see as leading practices for success in a Discussion Partner model.

Do not be dependent on one source for leads and referrals. You will gravitate toward the lead source that works best for you and your business. However, you should never become solely dependent on one channel. Leads can come from word of mouth, through lead providers, through social introductions, advertising, and many other opportunities.

Let's explore a few of the lead source programs that successfully worked in my own practice, and for hundreds of firms worldwide.

Do not be dependent on one source for leads and referrals.

Takeaway Questions:

1. Where do the majority of your leads come from right now?

2. What are some areas for lead sources you could be tapping into, but are currently not?

Actionable Item: Copy and paste the following onto your calendar!

Subject: The Importance of Lead Generation: Expanding My Lead Sources

Time Frame: 15 minutes

Notes: Identify 1-3 new areas in which you would like to expand your lead sourcing.

Next Steps: For each of these areas, create a strategy with benchmarks so that you can mark your progress toward your goals.

session 1

The Self-Generated Lead

There is no lead more important to me than a self-generated lead. This is somebody that I decided I wanted to meet and get to know—to form a relationship with, in order to start a journey with them. What's the goal of this journey? For me to become their gateway to all things insurance and financial services.

Now, I'm going to talk about buying leads, third-party vendors, information, and more. I've said, "The one with the most information wins," but we need to apply that to leads. I want to know everything about the person before I start to engage them in the relationship. What does this look like? It could be that I create a lead because I drive by a business or see a car with a sign on it, and I think, "That's a person I want to know." Then, I start to get background information on that person—today, this is easily attainable.

Back when I started in business, in the eighties, you'd drive by a business or see a car, and you'd have to go into the phone book or the newspaper to find information about them. There wasn't a lot of information to be had. Today, with a push of a button, you can know just about anything about anybody, because of the information highway. So as I look at somebody—whether they're a contractor, doctor, retail worker, hospitality worker, and so on—I can know everything about them by simply putting their name into a contact record and beginning to fill in those blanks.

The one with the most information wins.

What are the blanks? How to contact them; how best to communicate with them, if they're on social media...you get the idea. We call this appending data. We start appending information on that lead. The one with the most information wins. What other information can you gather? The charities they're involved in; the school they went to; the associations they're involved in—the church, synagogue, or mosque they attend. If they're in the community, you want to know who they know and what they know—how to get introduced to them in a more favorable light.

Birds of a feather flock together. I can go onto their social media and get to know who they are based on which people and organizations they're associated with. Who do you know that they also know? You're looking for every piece of information possible, so that, when you enter into a relationship with them, you don't have to backfill any of that information. Get as much of it up front as you can.

Practical Application: Talk to Those with Whom You're Comfortable

If I owned a firm today, I would train people to talk to those whom they feel most comfortable with. Maybe they came from an agricultural background, or a transportation background. Pick an area where you feel the most comfort, and start getting information on all the people you meet in that field. It's easy for you talk to them; so, the more information you get, the more relaxed you'll be.

We've moved from a hard-selling world to a soft-selling world. You know the field you came from, and you know others in that field. It's easier for you to build relationships with those leads.

Takeaway Questions:

1. What's one piece of information that you're missing for a good portion of your leads? How can you begin to put a system in place for your team to append that information easily and simply?

2. Do you currently have a CRM or other electronic method to capture and retain client information? If so, how are you utilizing this program to its fullest?

3.What are the various backgrounds of you and your team? How can you maximize on the contacts you each already have?

Actionable Item: Copy and paste the following onto your calendar!

Subject: The Self-Generated Lead: Utilizing Current CRM/Digital File to its Fullest

Time Frame: 15 minutes

Notes: Determine the areas in which you are not fully utilizing your electronic file system. These areas could include customer data fields, reporting functions, tracking features, etc.

Next Steps: Define all fields that are a "must" for you and your team to collect on every household/business.

session 2

Third-Party Sourcing

I get a lot of questions regarding third-party sourcing: do I believe in third-party sourcing? Of course, I do. It speeds up the process. Would you pay somebody for a lead? Of course, you would—if you can make a profit on it (and append plenty of data for that lead).

I'm going to buy a third-part lead, because they'll cut through all the rigmarole and get me right to the type of person that has a propensity to do business with me—not somebody else.

So, I'm going to buy a third-party lead, because they'll cut through all the rigmarole and get me right to the type of person that has a propensity to do business with me—not somebody else. Remember, I'm a Discussion Partner; I'm not a transactional seller. I buy the lead that fits my profile, and then I start appending data to it.

Practical Application: Carefully Select Your Lead Providers

I like to go to conferences where the lead providers are, so I can listen to their thoughts on leads—both today and for the future. I need to discover which lead providers are going to provide me with leads that fit the Discussion Partner profile.

I'm not going to take all comers; but I'm going to be a student of leads. Become an expert at it, so that you can choose whom you do business with. Find a lead provider that can provide you with the ideal client—someone who has a high propensity to do business with you.

Takeaway Questions:

1. Which lead providers are your top sources at the moment? Are you satisfied with what you gain from them?

____

____

____

____

____

2. How many leads per month are you buying? What is your total budget each month for outsourcing for leads?

3.What is your current Return on Investment (ROI)?

Actionable Item: Copy and paste the following onto your calendar!

Subject: Third-Party Sourcing: ROI

Time Frame: 15 minutes

Notes: Are you currently getting the most from every lead you are purchasing? What data are you consistently appending? What data should you append that you are not currently appending?

Next Steps: Each month, calculate your ROI for each lead source. Determine if all of your lead sources are profitable and if you are gleaning and retaining the most possible from each lead.

session 3

Giving and Receiving

I love the philosophy from Jim Rohn that says, "Giving starts the receiving process." If people see you simply trying to sell...well, let's just say nobody likes a salesperson. They'll even tell you so. That's why the movie *Groundhog Day* was so funny. Remember Ned Ryerson? He was hilarious—because there was a little truth in it. That's the way people perceive us.

If you come across as a salesy person, nobody wants to do business with you. Now, I'm proud to sell. Whether I'm selling insurance or financial services, I'm proud of my profession. However, I don't want to come across as a hard seller. So, when I'm doing local marketing, I want to give first and then receive.

Who do I give to? It could be a charity or an event; however, throwing money at things isn't ideal. Truly giving—getting your hands dirty—that's what really makes a difference. The people who are involved in your community are the people who need the services you provide. When they see you as a giver, and not a taker, they'll naturally gravitate towards you.

Remember Ned Ryerson? He was hilarious—because there was a little truth in it. That's the way people perceive us.

Let me give you a couple of concepts that worked for me when I actually was in agency. I like to give back to the youth, because I believe that people love their kids—and youth are the future of our communities. There were a couple things that I did personally, including creating a Frisbee golf course, partnering with the city and some other folks who helped me do the heavy lifting. Not everybody uses it, of course; but it's free! Kids can use it—it's something for the whole family. You can throw events around things like this.

Giving away things like bicycles or jackets during Christmastime is another great option. There are all kinds of inventive things that you can do that are good—that help the community while telling people what you're about: the culture you bring as a giving business, not a taking one.

Practical Application: Get to Know People First

If you want to receive, you need to set yourself up to win. Get to know people. Remember that self-generated lead we talked about? Getting a business card is all it takes to start that lead. During events, if you can get marginal information about people in order to contact them later (not sell to them later, but just to start a relationship), you're ready to go.

It's setting yourself up to win, while remembering that you're there to give—not to take or to sell.

Takeaway Questions:

1. What events do you most like to frequent in order to meet (not sell to) people you don't know?

____

____

____

____

____

2. How are you giving back in practical, tangible ways to your community right now?

____

____

____

____

____

3. Are you capitalizing on your involvement through self-promotion via social media, your firm's website, local

advertising, etc.? How could you increase your involvement in these areas?

____

____

____

____

____

Actionable Item: Copy and paste the following onto your calendar!

Subject: Giving and Receiving: Community Involvement

Time Frame: 15 minutes

Notes: Research local events taking place in the upcoming year that you and your firm can be a part of.

Next Steps: Determine a budget and level of commitment (i.e. personal time, donations of products or funds, hosting capabilities, etc.) for each selected event.

session 4

Social Marketing Tactics

You know, there have been books written about social marketing tactics; there have been numerous talks about this, videos about it...I have to be honest with you: I missed the mark. Why? Because I didn't get in on the early stages of social marketing.

That doesn't mean I don't have a social presence—I always did. I love Facebook, LinkedIn, and similar platforms. But I never had it working for me. Again, I don't want to come across as a salesperson; so, I'm going to have my personal Facebook and a business Facebook. I'm going to have other forms of social media—YouTube, Instagram, a blog, and so on—different methods to communicate what I'm about.

If you're in personal distribution, you need to have a social strategy. It can't just be one thing; you've got to have a lot of lines in the water. You've got to be touching a lot of people. The reason I keep my personal accounts separate is that people want to see my personal life. They want to know that I'm a real human being. You can't just put fake things onto your personal account—that won't work. I like to put normal things—what I'm eating, what my family is up to, what my friends are doing. The strategy is as simple as, "Here's my personal life; and here's my business, which I'm proud of."

You've got to have a lot of lines in the water. You've got to be touching a lot of people.

Get a social media strategy. You may pay a third party to do this, or you may do it yourself. Either way, you've got to have it to compete in today's world. It's all about content, and it's all about information. Social media is the best way to distribute these things.

Practical Application: Outsource Social Media Services

When you're thinking about social media, be involved; but also, just like when you're hiring employees, there are parts of it you may want to outsource. Remember, be involved no matter what. You want to make sure you have a roadmap for your social media. If you hire somebody, it may be more cost-effective; but you still have to inspect what you expect.

Takeaway Questions:

1. What social media platforms are you active on right now? Which ones do you see the most return on investment from for your time and energy?

2. Do you outsource any of your social media content creation? Why or why not?

3. Are you consistent with your posts and updates? How do you know for sure?

____

____

____

4. Do you keep your personal and business accounts separate on social media? If not, you will want to separate these immediately.

____

____

____

____

____

Actionable Item: Copy and paste the following onto your calendar!

Subject: Social Marketing Tactics: Increasing Your Visibility

Time Frame: 15 minutes

Notes: Determine if all or part of your current social media accounts will be monitored and updated in-house, or outsourced. Do any new accounts need to be opened? Do any accounts need to be closed?

Next Steps: Regardless of your decision to handle your social media in house, or to outsource, set up consistent messaging across all platforms.

session 5

Maintaining Top-of-Mind Status

I learned early on that you must celebritize yourself. You don't want to be boastful; you want to have humility. But if you don't tell people who you are and what you are, nobody else is going to do it for you. You've got to have a strategy of celebritization.

Now, to do this, I'm going to make sure I know who all the influencers are in my marketplace. I want to make sure that my message is getting out. Because most people don't read the newspaper today, I'm using social media, word of mouth, and events. I'm telling people what I do, what I'm doing right, and how I'm helping the community. There's a strategy here.

Let me go back to the influencers. In your community, there's the chief of police; the clergy; people in charge of the Hispanic chamber...I could go on and on, but you get the idea.

There are influencers. They may not buy from you, but they need to know you. Remember, people buy from people they know and trust; and these influencers are those that people go to for advice.

I learned early on that you must celebritize yourself.

When others tell influencers that they've done business with your organization, the influencer will know who you are, and what you've done for the community. This is why it's so important to have a plan for how to let everyone know what you're doing. Once again, you want to do this in humility; but you need to let people know what you do. If you don't, nobody else is going to do it for you. Have a plan.

Practical Application: Have a Press Release

In the old days, people sent press releases to the newspaper, the radio station, and so on. We don't do that anymore, because those outlets are pretty much dead. With that being said, where does the press release go nowadays? To the influencers we've just talked about. If you won an award, or a team member got recognized by another organization or group, celebritize that.

Have a press release, send out a note that you'd like to recognize that individual (and why), and ask for help in congratulating them. That release goes out to all the influencers.

What press release can you get out today that tells the leaders in the community what's going on? Change the way you communicate your press release based on the communication channels that are thriving today.

Takeaway Questions:

1. What practical steps are you taking to celebritize yourself, and get the word out about you and your organization (i.e. an announcement of an award your firm won, bringing awareness to your involvement in local causes, etc.)?

____

____

____

____

____

2. When was the last time you created something akin to a press release? To whom did you send it?

____

____

____

____

____

3. Look for places that send electronic newsletters (i.e. Chamber of Commerce, church groups, leads groups, etc.) in which you can promote yourself and your firm.

____

____

____

____

____

Actionable Item: Copy and paste the following onto your calendar!

Subject: Maintaining Top-of-Mind Status: "Celebretizing" Your Firm

Time Frame: 15 minutes

Notes: What is something your firm has been recently recognized for? Begin developing a press release for this accomplishment.

Next Steps: Create a strategy to send a press release every quarter.

session 6

Staff and Lead Development

How is the staff involved in lead creation and appending data to leads? You want to hire people from different walks of life. Now, everyone still needs to sing from the same song sheet, as we discussed earlier. However, you want people with different skill sets, styles, and appeals.

I have more of a "New York" style way of speaking–quick, to the point, and efficient. I hired people into my agency who talked slowly, in a measured manner. Personally, that kind of speech would drive me up a wall; but some people don't like my style. They want a person who talks slowly. We'd hire people who rode Harleys–something I've never done. Why? Because people who ride motorcycles travel with people who ride motorcycles. There are a lot of business owners in that sphere. If I don't hire that person, I don't get those leads.

You can't be all things to all people; so, you need to look for people who have influence in different places than you. I don't attend every church in my community every Sunday; however, if I have ten different people on my team who attend ten different churches, I'm influencing people all over the community. So, we hire young and old; those in clubs; those who worship in different areas. We're spread out amongst the community.

You can't be all things to all people; so, you need to look for people who have influence in different places than you.

I want people who are involved, who can create leads and append data to those leads—data that's readily available in the marketplace.

Practical Application: Ask for 100 Names

Sit your team members down and ask them to write out 100 names of people they know. Do this without regard to whether you're already doing business with these individuals, or whether they're outside of your sphere. It will be difficult to think of 100 names, but each of your team members likely knows this many people (maybe not well; but we'll get to know them better).

These are people they touch in their places of worship; their clubs; their gyms; their schools; their neighborhoods.

We're looking for everybody they know that we *don't* know. Cities and towns are growing. There are tons of people in your area that you don't know. If you want to extend your reach, sit your staff down and ask them who they know.

Takeaway Questions:

1. List one area of expertise or influence that isn't currently represented on your team. Where could you begin to recruit someone in this sphere?

____

____

____

____

____

2. Do you regularly attend, or allow time for your team members to attend, leads groups meetings, professional gatherings, chambers, etc.?

____

____

____

____

____

Actionable Item: Copy and paste the following onto your calendar!

Subject: Staff & Lead Development: Leads Lists

Time Frame: 15 minutes

Notes: Work with your team to begin creating lists of their contacts, including, but not limited to, personal contacts, business contacts, religious group contacts, and professional development groups contacts. These contacts are not just for prospective clients but are also prospective employees, expertise partners, referral sources, and so on.

Next Steps: Continue growing these lists and creating customized marketing plans.

session 7

Systems and Assessments

I often get asked, "What type of CRM system should I use? What type of lead provider should I use? Can you give me an assessment, so I can know what to do?" The answer is there isn't just one. If there was, it would control the entire market. The key is to land on the best lead provider and CRM system for *your* organization.

If you're an exclusive agent, and your company provides you with a CRM system, that's what you're using. If you're an independent, or you have the opportunity to use multiple systems, then you're going to pick the one that best suits you and your business. I don't worry about the technology today because, with the marketplace, it keeps evolving and improving.

I utilize the CRM that I have today. Most of what I've seen as a consultant–working for carriers to implement new systems and execute the systems they have–is that CRM systems are completely deficient. In other words, most organizations haven't capitalized on the true capabilities of the CRM system they currently have. They haven't executed out in the field or in the ecosystem as completely as they can.

What is the best CRM? The one that you use 100%.

The first step, then, is to do an assessment of your own purview. If you have empty slots in your leads– "work phone," "email," and so on–they need to be filled. You need to append that data. From the person's occupation to where they have other policies, fill all the blanks in.

Don't worry about getting the latest evolution of your CRM. I see a lot of great CRMS that aren't used to their full potential. What is the best CRM? The one that you use 100%. If you don't put the information in, it can't be used.

Practical Application: Fill in the Blanks

It's likely that you aren't populating the information into your CRM to the fullest extent. It's likely you haven't completely populated the leads you already have. You need to sit down and do an assessment of your current situation. How are you going to populate it as fast as possible? A year from now isn't soon enough—a new evolution will come along by then.

Things populate faster today, as systems change and migrate. It's a constant state of flux. However, if there's no information in the system, there's nothing to keep moving forward. Fill in the blanks!

Takeaway Questions:

1. How updated is your technology? Do you need to upgrade or subscribe to the latest evolution of the CRM you're currently using?

---

2. If you are required to use a carrier/company legacy system, what can you layer on top of it to make it more effective?

Actionable Item: Copy and paste the following onto your calendar!

Subject: Systems and Assessments: Assessing Current CRM

Time Frame: 15 minutes

Notes: Assess your current CRM. Is it ample enough to fit your current and future needs? Are you utilizing it to streamline your business? Can everyone on your team access it? Does everyone use it consistently and uniformly?

Next Steps: Set up a timeframe to upgrade or convert CRM programs, if necessary. Continue to get everyone on your team to use your firm's CRM in a more consistent manner.

session 8:

The Introduction

Set time for yourself each day to physically go on four introduction appointments and make four introduction calls to set appointments for the next day. Go to these appointments on your way to work, on your way to and from lunch, or on your way home from work. Take with you a small cake or candy along with a business card.

These appointments should last no more than five minutes each (remember, you are just introducing yourself so the person can get familiar with your name and face). You should never turn your introductory appointment into a selling interview.

After your face-to-face meeting, put your prospect on your calendar for a follow-up call the next day (call and thank the prospect for taking the time to meet with you). Add this person to your "drip" marketing program to begin receiving letters from your office – part of your ongoing efforts to keep your name and what you offer in front of customers. Keep each prospect on your calendar for another follow-up call in approximately two weeks. This time when you call, ask those prospects if you can start a file on them.

You should never turn your introductory appointment into a selling interview.

Once you have personal and/or business insurance information from prospects, you will want to put reminders on your calendar to follow up with them at the "right" time. For example, if you know their auto policy renews on June 1, you will want to call on May 1 to just say "Hi" and see how things are going. Chances are, they just received their renewal notice and will want to talk to you about it. However, do not pounce on prospects—these should be relaxed calls.

If you are unable to obtain an appointment, put them back on the calendar to make contact at the next renewal, and so on. Never take any prospect off of your calendar (unless the person specifically requests it).

Practical Application: The Introduction

How do you position yourself? It all starts with your introduction. People buy from people they know and trust. If they consider you the gateway to all things insurance and financial services, they'll buy from you. Target people who fit into your practice, both in topic and in geography. Start by bringing in candy and just getting to know people—don't sell at first. Then, eventually, when the time comes for them to buy products or services, you'll be in the forefront of their minds.

Takeaway Questions

1. Create a list of 20 businesses you could visit this week to introduce yourself.

____

____

____

____

____

2. Have key staff make a list of 20 businesses they could each visit to make an introduction.

____

____

____

____

____

2. Prepare marketing materials to have on hand for introduction visits. Get creative. Make sure they are always branded or contain a business card.

____

____

____

____

____

Actionable Item: Copy and paste the following onto your calendar!

Subject: The Introduction Program: Creating a Sustainable Plan

Time Frame: 15 minutes

Notes: Email support@korsgaden.com for a complimentary copy of their Introduction Program outline and script template.

Next Steps: Customize these templates for your personal business needs. Continue to identify and visit (and revisit) 20 businesses each week.

Module 6: The Customer Journey

introduction

The Customer Journey

All right—now that we're committed to getting a 360° view of the customer, to being the gateway to all things insurance and financial services, in this section, we're going to talk about the customer journey: from getting to know the customer, to setting up the presentation, to achieve success and product density—having more products and services in every household and business that we serve.

Takeaway Questions:

1. How many prospective clients, on average, are you and your team meeting with each week?

____

____

____

____

____

2. Create client appointment goals for your firm. Include goals for new clients, existing clients, prospect introductions, etc.

____

____

____

____

____

Actionable Item: Copy and paste the following onto your calendar!

Subject: The Customer Journey: Client Meeting Goals

Time Frame: 15 minutes

Notes: Determine the number of appointments each person in your office should have each week. Share these with your team and create a plan to achieve these goals.

Next Steps: Inspect what you expect. Spend time weekly to determine if goals were met, what the closing ratio for your firm is, ways to improve, and so on.

session 1

The First Contact

Now, let's talk about the first contact. I gave you some ideas earlier on the introduction program: introducing yourself and the service you provide. Most people want someone to guide them. They don't want to be sold, and they don't want to be told; but they want someone that they know and trust to give them advice on matters that they know nothing about.

And most people you meet don't have the time to research and get to know all their options on insurance and financial services. Your first call is just to get them to be relaxed—to get to know you. In subsequent calls, you will get to know them deeper and deeper, until that moment comes—whether it's on the third call, the fifth call, or maybe even the sixth or seventh call—where you come in, you're saying hello, and they actually approach you and say, "Hey, I'd love to talk to you about life insurance. I'd love to talk to you about my auto and home insurance. I'd love to talk to you about my business insurance."

Your first call is just to get them to be relaxed—to get to know you. In subsequent calls, you will get to know them deeper and deeper.

You've set it up, so they *ask* you to do business with you. But remind them that you were just coming by to say hello; you'd like to set up a time, under the right conditions, to get to know them better so you can show them how you help people in situations similar to theirs.

Practical Application: Ask Questions and Document Information

Now, you've positioned yourself to get the client to come in and meet with you under the right conditions. You can get them to relax, so you can ask them questions and get a 360° view of their family and/or business. This is very important: if you're selling auto insurance, and you don't know what their assets are, it's hard to prescribe a limit. If they are having you deal with their assets and their life insurance, but you don't know what their auto insurance is, you're not giving them the advice they need to protect what they have before they start building into the future.

Can you see how it all intertwines? You can't do anything without knowing everything. Now, you've positioned yourself. The customer comes into your office. You ask them the appropriate questions. If you're an exclusive agency, you have the systems and tools that you need; if you're an independent agency, or a direct writer, you also have the tools you need.

The first thing you need to do is make sure you have an easy way to ask questions and document the information into a system where you can get a complete view of the customer, everything they have to protect, and everything they have to grow their assets.

Takeaway Questions:

1. Do you have a "new client" procedure in place for your first appointment? This should include materials such as, but not be limited to, a business brochure ("About" sheet), a client profile sheet, a product spectrum, etc. What do you need to add to this procedure?

____

____

____

____

____

2. What is your procedure for capturing all the information you've gleaned, and creating workflows from your initial client meeting?

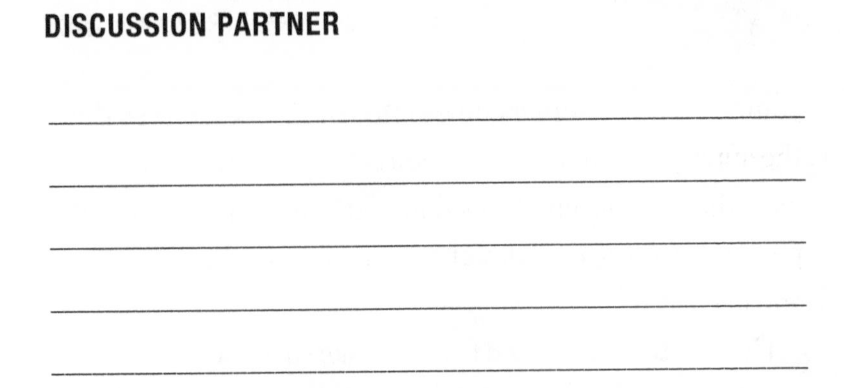

Actionable Item: Copy and paste the following onto your calendar!

Subject: The First Contact: Creating a New Client Meeting Template

Time Frame: 15 minutes

Notes: Compile a New Client Meeting file to contain all documents needed to glean personal and business information during the initial meeting with a client.

Next Steps: Ensure that every desk is set up with electronic and printed copies of the New Client Meeting templates.

session 2

Closing on the First Call

The next question is, "Do I close on the first call?" I was brought up in an environment where, yes, you closed on the first call if you were selling auto; you closed on the first call if you were selling property insurance; and, if appropriate, you closed on your business insurance the same way.

However, we take a cue from the life-only agents; the big business writers of insurance; the financial services agents—they all get to know the client. They're more laid back. They want to know more about the client so that, when they present, they present the right product, and a higher value proposition.

We need to lay that same importance on providing a high value proposition with auto, home, umbrella, specialty products, health insurance...you need to get to know the client better, so you can get them the type of service and advice that they need. I'm not for closing on the first sale. However, if you work in an exclusive environment, or you're an independent agent or direct writer, there are processes that require that you close on the first call.

You need to get to know the client better, so you can get them the type of service and advice that they need.

I'm an advocate to do dual marketing programs until you get to the Discussion Partner model. I go right to the Discussion Partner model; but you may want to simply wean yourself off the first call close for now.

Practical Application: Dual Models

You can do both if you have proper staffing. Remember, you can create a business within your business. What do I mean by this? If I'm charged with closing on the first call for auto, and I need more auto, I can assign that to someone, and make them accountable. I don't stop what made me successful. I create a whole new business within my business—I don't have to go out and buy a new shop; I just plant a new one within my operation. It's called the Discussion Partner Model.

So now, as I attract new customers outside of the system I was working in, I have a dual program going; and eventually, as I look at my model, I ask myself, "Which model is getting me the most sales, with the bigger returns on investment, and better retention. Which model is ultimately giving far greater service to my customer?" Remember, the customer is in control. Put the customer first, and then the commission and revenues come. It's magical.

Takeaway Questions:

1. Who could you immediately assign to do "transactional" selling only in your firm for two weeks? If you have no employees, can you assign yourself to this on alternating days?

____

____

____

____

____

2. Create a way to catalogue the results of the transactional meetings and the Discussion Partner meetings. Include the number of appointments/presentations, the close ratio, the number of lines written per household, premiums, and any other factors you would like to track.

____

____

DISCUSSION PARTNER

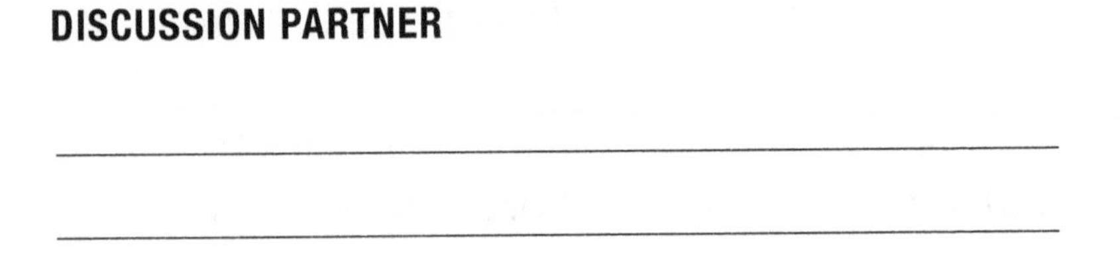

Actionable Item: Copy and paste the following onto your calendar!

Subject: Closing on the First Call: Dual Marketing Programs

Time Frame: 15 minutes

Notes: Determine a start date and who will participate in a trial dual marketing program in your firm.

Next Steps: Evaluate the results in two weeks. Should the trial continue for additional evaluation, or should you begin operating under one marketing program?

session 3

Quoting Tactics

I don't want to have my gravestone say, "He gave the best quotes." I want it to say, "He gave the greatest service to the people he served." With that in mind, quoting is important, because it's part of the presentation. Remember, if you give enough presentations, you'll give enough quotes.

Many of the carriers I represent measure quotes, because there's a ratio: statistics show that if I quote 100, I'm going to get 20 sales in property and casualty and auto and fire. In business, the ratios are a little different; but you get the idea. If I know what the ratios are, and I want to give a lot of auto quotes, I just need to step up my presentations for Discussion Partner households and businesses.

A presentation to a household with a business has a lot of quoting opportunity underneath that the customer doesn't see. Somebody's doing the quote; but the presentation is more powerful if it's not merely, "Here's your coverage, here's your price."

What you want to do is focus on the presentation, not on the quotes.

Instead, it needs to be, "Here's how I'm going to protect you. Here's how I'm going to serve you." Again, they're not going to buy on that ratio every time. If we give 100 quotes in auto and we get 20, we lost 80. Applying that same thing to the presentation, our ratio goes up, because they're buying the package. So, what you want to do is focus on the presentation, not on the quotes. The quotes have to be done as part of the presentation.

Practical Application: Try Both Methods

Here's a hot tip as you transform and transition into presentations versus quotes. Remember, you'll still give a lot of quotes by giving a lot of presentations. So, you're hitting your quota behind the scenes. It's a numbers game.

But I want you to do this: have a control group that just does transactional quoting—not presentations. "Here's your coverage, here's your price. You want it? Buy it." And then have another group, or person, who is not part of that control group, start giving Discussion Partner presentations. From the presentations, start to create a ratio—the close rate for presentations versus the close rate for transactions.

Measure and monitor these two and find out which one brings you more profit as a business. With presentations, you're thinking about the customer, and the commissions come. With transactions, you're just thinking about making commission. Make sure you measure and monitor both and decide which one works best for you. I know which one you're going to pick.

Takeaway Questions:

1. Are your close ratios within the national average of 20%? If they are lower, what can you change to increase them? If they are higher, how can you capitalize on this success?

2. Is your office meeting/connecting with enough clients and prospects each day for a proper analysis? If not, how can you immediately increase your reach?

Actionable Item: Copy and paste the following onto your calendar!

Subject: Quoting Tactics: Monitoring Close Ratios

Time Frame: 15 minutes

Notes: Catalogue the number of quotes given each day over the next week and find the combined total for your firm. Evaluate the close ratio based off the total of all quotes given. What is this ratio?

Next Steps: Implement new ideas to help increase your close ratios.

session 4

Bundling

Let's talk about bundling. You see commercials on TV in which agents say, "Let me bundle this for you—your auto and your home." Up until now, the industry has primarily focused their efforts on bundling just auto and home (renters). The Discussion Partner Model takes bundling to a whole new level. It's bundling everything.

A 360° view allows you to offer everything from Day 1. You're going to bundle from the start: auto, home, umbrella, life—decide what's appropriate, but bundle it all. Bundling is more than just offering a discount; it's looking at everything in the household and/or business to ensure that all coverages and limits are properly aligned across all policies.

Now, you can't sell them everything in one day; but you're going to speed the process up, because you're never going to stop advising them until they've made a decision on everything. "I was able to take care of your auto, your home, and your life today, but we need you to come back in. I need to talk to you about the business we discussed. I want to be respectful of your time, but I'm sure you agree it's important. I was able to help you over here with advice; I want to help you with advice on your business."

You're offering them multiple products and services; they'll decide what's best for them.

Again, it's a bundle. You're offering them multiple products and multiple services; and they'll decide what's best for them.

Practical Application: Create a Bigger Bundle

Whether you're a direct writer, an agent selling a product, an independent agent in a firm, or an exclusive agent, we all have the opportunity to bundle. We're all selling a package. The question is, are we going to keep trying to do bundles of auto and home only? If you never go deeper with the household, you risk waking up ten years from now with still only the auto and home. Or worse, you risk somebody else offering the client a better bundle and stealing away the auto and home that you have. I've got to tell you, the life-only agents and the financial-services-only agents are coming after your business. You may not make a commission on every product; but the minute somebody else gets in the door, they're going to go after everything else.

Now, with advanced technology, more buying options, and new competitors, the need to bundle is more important than ever. Create a bundle that's bigger than what you offer today. Remember, you're going to do it in chunks; you're not going to wait six months, a year, or two years from now, hoping they bring everything to you. You're going to demand it by starting the bundle process in a much bigger fashion.

Takeaway Questions:

1. What percentage of your current book of business is monoline? What percentage is just auto and home? Create a strategy to "bundle" these existing clients.

____

____

____

____

____

2. Create a strategy to educate your team and your clients about why "bundling" information is important—even if they are not in the market to buy all products and services from your firm.

____

____

DISCUSSION PARTNER

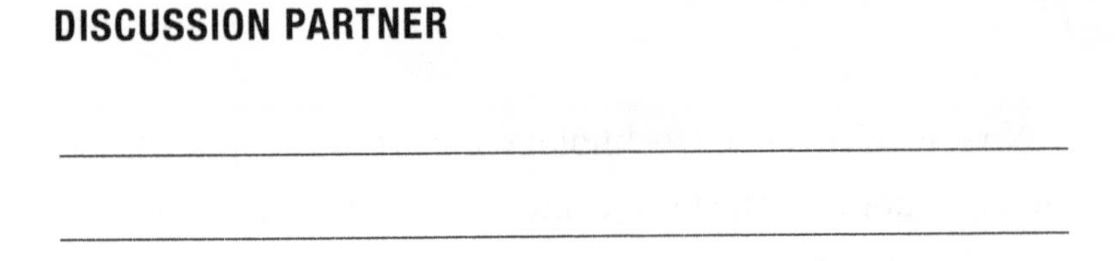

Actionable Item: Copy and paste the following onto your calendar!

Subject: Bundling: Bundling Current Clients

Time Frame: 15 minutes

Notes: Create a marketing strategy to meet with all current clients who have either monoline or just auto and home with your firm.

Next Steps: Continue to prioritize this client list to meet with all clients over a determined time frame.

session 5

The Package Presentation

Here's where we have to look at the system, we're under. Many of you work in the independent world, and you represent multiple carriers. Some of you are tied to exclusive companies, and that's awesome. Some of you are with direct writers that have transactional selling—and that's okay, too. We're all in the same ballgame; it's just that some of us are in a different inning. Each model has their own advantages and disadvantages. The key is to focus on your advantages.

The key is to look at what's available—because of the systems and the processes on the computer, you have to answer the questions the right way to get the appropriate coverage and cost for the consumer. A lot of our presentation is going to be built around the systems and processes of those we represent—either individually or multiple carriers.

In the case of multiple products and bundling, there are a lot of different things to ask, and a lot of different things to present. So, let's focus on presentation. There needs to be one, unified way for you to communicate with your customer. You must be compliant, and you must give them transparency in everything you discuss.

There needs to be one, unified way for you to communicate with your customer.

You have to give them what they need. This is where you need to dig in. As a consultant and a former practitioner, I have worked with many carriers to create these systems. The ones that I see that work, when they get down to the customer level, are the ones that are simple—they're easy to understand, and they're visually acceptable and appropriate when you're talking to the customer.

So, with that in mind, I'm going to ask you to dig down deep and assess everything that you have, and then roll it up into one way to communicate with your customer.

Practical Application: Look at Other Industries

Look at other industries and the way they present their products. Now, remember, we're not living in a hard-selling world anymore. We're living in an advice and content age—where you give information to people. How you communicate that message is important.

Takeaway Questions:

1. Do you currently practice your presentation? Take time to schedule a roleplay with your team and teach them ways to give a powerful and educational presentation.

____

____

____

____

____

2. What are the current techniques you use to help relax your client and set a conversational tone? Does your current style elicit information from your client? Don't just read down a list. Learn ways and techniques to engage your client for more in-depth responses.

____

____

____

____

____

Actionable Item: Copy and paste the following onto your calendar!

Subject: The Package Presentation: A Relaxed Presentation

Time Frame: 15 minutes

Notes: Define techniques and styles to roleplay with your team on how to conduct presentations to elicit the most information from your client.

Next Steps: Continue to hone these techniques and styles to create seamless presentations.

session 6:

A Proper Needs Assessment

As part of the 360° view of the customer, their family, and their business, we need to do a proper needs assessment. As we get to know them, we need to ask them the right questions. A comprehensive needs assessment should include everything the client has today, along with what their goals are for the future. Your job, as their Discussion Partner, is to create a plan to assist them with bridging the two. We can go back in time and take life insurance as an example.

It's the best example I know, because I'm a product of life insurance. My father bought life insurance a few months before he died, and left my family with enough money to live comfortably–not rich; but enough to pay off the house, and for everybody to go to college that wanted to go. My mom went back to work when we were in high school. But life insurance did exactly what it needed to do for us.

> We need to look at the big picture for everyone by doing a proper needs analysis.

Now, quite frankly, that was luck. Flash forward, and the life insurance business has evolved into a needs-analysis-based product. As we get to know the customer in a 360° view, that proper needs analysis can be applied to tell you exactly how much life insurance they may need. And the same thing is true in financial services, if you're licensed to do that. We need to apply this same process to business insurance, personal auto and home insurance, umbrella, health insurance... we need to look at the big picture for everyone by doing a proper needs analysis.

So, where do you start? You may represent one company; you may represent multiple companies. You may be a tight agent—exclusive—but there are libraries of needs analysis templates. My advice, having worked in the business for many years, is to take them all and create something that comfortably allows you to ask questions to the customer, and put that information into a program that will then prescribe coverages and services.

Practical Application: Assess Needs Analysis

Assess all the needs analyses you can find. Because of the Internet, and because of your relationship with different peers in our business, just ask. Ask everybody for their best needs analysis. You'd be surprised how many different versions I get. The key is to make your needs analysis thorough to the 360° view. Gather up everything that you can get and decide what you need to give your customer.

Takeaway Questions:

1. What are you currently using to collect needs assessment information from your clients? Does it include what their future wants, needs and goals will be?

____

____

____

____

____

2. When was the last time you conducted a needs assessment on your own household? The best way to determine if the assessment you are using (or creating) is as comprehensive as possible is to start by conducting an assessment on yourself. Tip: Have each of your team members do this for themselves. It will help them to understand why this

information is important, and how it can be used to better serve your customers.

____

____

____

____

____

Actionable Item: Copy and paste the following onto your calendar!

Subject: A Proper Needs Assessment: Creating a Comprehensive Needs Analysis

Time Frame: 15 minutes

Notes: Create or refine your current needs analysis to include all assets currently owned, short term/long term goals, and your recommendations on how to bridge these.

Next Steps: Ensure that all this information is catalogued in the client file, and that you continue to build on it with every meeting.

Module 7: Closing and Follow-Up

introduction

Closing and Follow-Up

Now we want to talk about closing and follow-up. Remember, we're not selling hard. We're soft-selling—that's really important. That means you're a Discussion Partner. You're not trying to sell every time you're talking to someone.

However, you've got to close the deal. They've got to agree that you are their gateway to all things insurance and financial services. Once you get them to agree to that, whether they initially buy product(s) from you or not, they still always come to you for advice. They always come to you for a review. They always get touched throughout the year, because you, your firm, your company, and your carrier(s) are their gateway to all things insurance and financial services.

Someone who knows the value of what they do is not afraid of not getting the commission every time; but they want to control the customer gateway—that way, they get the opportunity both today, and in the future. The key is to close the deal—to gain the opportunity—to be that gateway.

> Someone who knows the value of what they do is not afraid of not getting the commission every time; but they want to control the customer gateway.

Takeaway Questions:

1. What is your current closing ratio on presentations/ quotes? What factors do you think have contributed to it being what it is right now?

____

____

____

____

____

2. What is your current multiline closing ratio? How about monoline? What factors do you think have contributed to them being what they are right now (good or bad)?

____

____

Actionable Item: Copy and paste the following onto your calendar!

Subject: Closing and Follow-Up

Time Frame: 15 minutes

Notes: Determine what your current monoline and multiline closing ratios are. Create a plan to increase your multiline closing ratio by 1%, 3%, 5%, etc., over the next 12 months.

Next Steps: Assess your numbers monthly to determine if you are on track with your goals.

session 1

Knowing When to Close

How do you know when to close? Well, the first thing you need to have is all the information. If you're trying to close before you have the information, you're going back to the old way of doing business, which is transactional selling—putting it in a silo and hoping for the rest.

We're not going to hope for the rest. We're having conversations with someone, and they're feeling comfortable with us. Now, you need to lean into them and tell them why you do business the way you do. You want to be their advisor. You want to be their Discussion Partner, and you recognize they're not going to buy every product or every service from you.

In some cases, you may not even have a product to sell them. Aviation, equine coverage...maybe you don't sell health insurance. Maybe you don't offer financial services...but you explain that you have expert partners who do. You tee it up; you'll be there to help them make the decisions that are best for them and their family; but you'll always have competent, licensed professionals as your expertise partners. It could be people on your payroll, or people outside your organization. But again, you're not referring them over; you're bringing the expertise partner in. So how do you get the close? You explain what you do, and you explain how you get compensated. You're transparent, and then you ask to be their Discussion Partner.

How do you get the close? You explain what you do, and how you get compensated. You're transparent.

Practical Application: Test out the Discussion Partner Model

When I'm working with carriers, the nugget that I give them is this: Let's look at some of your agents at different points in their career. They may have been in the business for ten years, twenty years, thirty years, or three months. Let's ask them to position themselves as a Discussion Partner in a conversation with a customer. Don't try to sell them anything—just explain the type of service you offer to clients in situations similar to theirs.

Then I say, "Come back to me and report what the reaction was from the customer." It's always positive. Most people want somebody they can talk freely with; but they usually enter into the conversation guarded. All their life, they've been told not to trust salespeople. Most people are relieved when you tell them what you do, and that they're not expected to buy everything from you. Remember, you're not a professional visitor, so make it clear that you're for profit; you're not a nonprofit. Still, you're putting service first, and the commission second.

Takeaway Questions:

1. What do you struggle with most when closing a sale? What do you excel at?

____

____

____

____

____

2. Do you practice and roleplay closing scenarios for yourself and with your team? How could you integrate this into your weekly or monthly schedule?

____

____

DISCUSSION PARTNER

____

____

____

Actionable Item: Copy and paste the following onto your calendar!

Subject: When to Close

Time Frame: 15 minutes

Notes: Set time for you and your team to roleplay closing scenarios.

Next Steps: Continue to hone these techniques for a seamless closing procedure.

session 2

Seven Touch Points a Year

From here, the journey requires that we create a systematic way to touch our customer. Remember, I like seven times. You might like five; you might like three. But seven has worked for me, and the people I work with—both carriers and their distributors locally.

Seven seems to be the magic number. Remember, not every touch is offering a product. Some of the touches could be a thank you. Some of the touches could be an event marketing offering throughout the year.

However, we need to touch our customers seven times a year. It's all about follow-up. We need our staff to be efficient, and we need everything to happen automatically as much as possible. There is not a system in place where everything happens without a push of the button. But the more you don't have to push the button, the less chance for error; the less chance for a customer to fall through the cracks; the less chance there is that we don't follow up. And follow-up is everything.

We need to touch our customers seven times a year. It's all about follow up.

We want to put our workflow in place the minute we get the agreement from the customer: "You are the gateway to all things insurance and financial services." Based on our assessment, based on the needs, whatever we start with, we're immediately going into the next step.

The reason we never got product density as an industry is because we just kept waiting for it to happen. The time to step in is now, and make sure that we get that product density that completes the 360° view.

Practical Application: Pay Attention to Cues

People tend to give you cues as you're talking to them: what they have the most interest in. When I'm doing my consulting, I'll walk into a room, and I'll ask, "What's pressing out there right now?" Believe me, it changes from month to month, from year to year—the needs are changing all the time; and the same thing is true for your customers.

What's pressing to them? They'll tell you if you ask. "My kids are going to college—I need to save money." "My business needs more ways to protect itself, because I'm more liable for things than I used to be." It's *their* hot button—not yours. Make sure that you take cues from the customer and focus on what is most important to them.

Takeaway Questions:

1. Who can you assign immediately to begin adding marketing workflows to each of your current households? The goal is to have a minimum of seven ongoing workflows.

____

____

____

____

____

2. What is your product density on your current book of business? What product/service are you highest in? What product/service are you lowest in?

____

____

____

____

____

Actionable Item: Copy and paste the following onto your calendar!

Subject: Seven Touch Points a Year: Creating Workflows

Time Frame: 15 minutes

Notes: Create a plan to add seven ongoing and open workflows for every client you currently are doing business with. Make it a standard operating procedure (SOP) to add seven ongoing and open workflows for all new clients.

Next Steps: From names A – Z, block time each week to ensure your entire book of business is receiving seven touches through open workflows.

session 3

Great Claims Experiences

One of the best things that can happen to deepen your relationship with your customer is for them to have a great claims experience. It could be their house; their car; their business. God forbid it's a life policy...but you want to be there at the time they need you most.

Anybody can give you a bill, and anybody can mess it up. But, at a time they need you most—like the death of a loved one, or the burning down of a building—whether it's personal or business—your customer is walking through a traumatic experience.

There's so much going on in the world. The news is a maze of madness. You're getting messages on the economy being up or down; you're getting political messages; you're getting business messages. The world is changing, and the information that's out there can be disconcerting—even overwhelming. Pile a loss on top of that...and the bottom line is that your customers need you. They need, and want, you to hold their hand through the maze of madness. That's the best service you can give; and then, coming out of that place, it's the best time to restate your value, and to do another 360° view to keep it up-to-date. When you've paid a claim, they need to recognize the big catastrophe that could have happened. Now, they believe.

People have zero tolerance for ineffective service. It's your time to shine; it's your time to live up to the promise you made them.

The other thing about enduring a loss is this: people have zero tolerance for ineffective service. It's your time to shine; it's your time to live up to the promise you made them when they started doing business with you. Perception is so important. Don't assume they know that you paid $100,000, or $200,000 (or, in my case, back when I was practicing insurance, I had one loss in which the grand total was 14 million dollars). You've got to remind your client, year after year after year. The same client that would take the $500,000 or a million dollars, if they're not thinking about it, is the same client that could leave you in order to save $20.

People will pay more for value; but value is a perception. Don't assume they know the true value you're offering them. Step up and give them the type of service they desire and have every right to expect during a claim. Then, tell them what you're doing for them.

Practical Application: Follow Up After Claims

I have a good friend in Michigan who pulls losses to help his agency team members and field leaders. He looks at the losses and goes back out to talk to the clients, to make sure they were happy with the service they received on their claims.

This is a positive experience for him almost always; it also frequently leads to a conversation about additional products and services. This "over the top" service can help you pour gas on the fire. Make a list of all your claims that have recently closed. Go out and shake their hand and ask them if they were satisfied with the service you provided.

Takeaway Questions:

1. How involved is your office in the claims process? Do you assign an internal team member to handle it, or refer it out to a claims center?

____

____

____

____

____

2. What are 3–5 strategies you can immediately implement to set your claims service apart from your competition (i.e. personal on-site visits, dedicated phone lines or email addresses, dedicated team members, etc.)?

____

____

____

____

____

Actionable Item: Copy and paste the following onto your calendar!

Subject: Follow Up After Claims: Personal Touch

Time Frame: 15 minutes

Notes: Pull a list of all currently closed claims for the past 30, 60, and 90 days. Set time to personally follow up with each—preferably in person, when possible.

Next Steps: Implement strategies going forward for your office to have a more personal approach to the claims process.

session 4

Benchmark Everything

Benchmark everything. We've studied growing agencies. The difference between the winners and those that remain stagnant is that the winners benchmark everything.

Benchmark how many people you meet; benchmark how many people you follow up with to get to know; benchmark if those connections turn into real relationships; benchmark how many presentations you give; benchmark how many sales were made by line; benchmark how much premium came in; benchmark what your follow up is.

Successful agencies benchmark everything.

Successful agencies benchmark everything. Here's another thing they benchmark, groups of people. If you're hot in writing the medical field, double down. If you're hot in writing hospitality as a vocation, double down. If it's approaching businesses, double down...one of the biggest doors into a household is the garage door; but an even bigger door is their business—it's a money machine.

Benchmark everything.

Practical Application: Put the Information In

Here's an idea you can implement immediately. I don't care what your CRM system is—who created it, if it's homegrown, out of the box, or off the shelf. I don't care whether your company provides it. We need to put the information in.

Create a benchmarking system within your technology. Maybe you need to do it on an Excel spreadsheet to start. I've found, in a lot of these technologies with multiple carriers—or direct or exclusive carriers—somewhere in the system is a place to put information that you can draw out.

If that information, those analytics, are important enough, I guarantee you that the carrier or the CRM supplier will make it easier for you. Start benchmarking everything immediately.

Takeaway Questions:

1. Do you currently have benchmarks set up for each area of your business? Do you benchmark by line item or department? Does it include all payroll, including yourself?

2. What are your minimum goals for each? What are your stretch (or over-the-top) goals?

Actionable Item: Copy and paste the following onto your calendar!

Subject: Benchmark Everything: Business Assessment

Time Frame: 15 minutes

Notes: Create or refine your benchmarking tools for each line item of your business.

Next Steps: Audit your numbers often to ensure you are staying on track.

session 5

Selling Skills

Now that we're training people and helping them with the Discussion Partner model, your team may ask, "Do I still work on my selling skills?" Of course, you do. Just like you work on your approach skills, you need to work on your selling skills. It's different than it was when I first started, because objection handling was intended to "go for the kill"—that's what they called it.

We're not going for the kill; but we do have to handle objections, because they're there. It could be limitations on coverage; it could be cost. It could be the services you provide. Today, there's different versions of policies. There used to be one-size-fits-all; now you can get a stripped-down policy in some cases, for some products. Some are high-end, and some are policies that don't intend to even pay all claims—they even tell you that.

You need to know your product; but you also need to know the buying signals from the customer, and what they want. In my view, you always sell the best at the best cost; because the worst time to figure out what kind of insurance you have is at the time of a loss. I like to get all objections out of the way by bringing them up before the client does.

I like to get all objections out of the way by bringing them up before the client does.

The biggest objection is going to be whether they want you to handle everything or not. Again, we go back to bringing that up, and positioning yourself so there's an agreement between you and your client that you are the gateway to all things insurance and financial services.

Practical Application: Go Get Information

If you want to learn how to talk to people and close sales, have all the information you can get. You can Google it or get it on YouTube. A good example of this is my brother—he's a really good guitar player, and one day, he said to me, "I used to buy lots of sheet music, and I would sit there trying to figure everything out. You can pretty much search any song you want, and they'll give it to you." Within seconds, he knows how to play it, because he knows how to transfer that information and make it real.

You can do the same thing. Remember, don't just look at insurance and financial services. If you want to learn how to be great at selling in today's world, go out and listen to talks on selling in today's world. The information's already been created. You just need to go out and get it.

Takeaway Questions:

1. What are some of the most common objections you hear? What about your team? How are these currently being handled?

____

____

____

____

____

2. Do you currently have a strategy in place to bring up objections first when meeting with clients? If so, what is it? If not, spend some time developing one.

____

____

____

____

____

Actionable Item: Copy and paste the following onto your calendar!

Subject: Selling Skills: Objection Handling

Time Frame: 15 minutes

Notes: Create scripts/word tracks for you and your team to use when handling objections with clients.

Next Steps: Continue to hone these scripts/word tracks, keeping in mind that objections are often driven by current world affairs.

session 6

What Needs to Happen Next?

I like to have a checklist of everything that needs to happen next. Once the customer has said that you're the gateway to all things insurance and financial services—once you've actually shown them a presentation and they start to buy product from you—you're now taking notes on everything that happened in that transaction. You're still being mindful that you have a 360° view—your job is not one transaction; it's to provide advice on everything: even those products and services that you don't offer as an agent.

This requires a lot of notetaking. There needs to be a checklist, a system, a process, to make sure everything is getting done, so that nothing falls through the cracks. I'll say it a hundred times: notes are one of the most important things. If you don't make a note, it didn't happen. Whoever gets to that

CRM note knows what happened last. They know if there was a billing issue; they know if there was a claim issue; they know if the person needs a certain product or service. The note is so important.

There needs to be a checklist, a system, a process, to make sure that everything is getting done, so that nothing falls through the cracks.

The next step is also important: setting up workflows. We set up a generic workflow for them; but now, we're going to drill it down because, in our last interaction, we decided that they needed an umbrella, or excess insurance, or life insurance. We now change the workflow to include that—that's the next step. Everything else keeps going (or maybe we delete something); but we've got to put in that next step.

That checklist makes sure that we do it; and then, when we put it into the computer, the checklist goes away, and the computer reminds us of what needs to happen next.

Practical Application: Create Workflows for Your Products

Let's use life insurance as our example for a checklist and planning what happens next. If you sell life insurance—if you're licensed, or you have somebody on your team that does it—there are certain things that need to happen. We get the sale, we get the application, we get the check. But it needs to go to underwriting. It needs to have a medical ordered. It needs to have doctors' attending physician reports. Whatever your company or companies require, there needs to be a checklist for all of this—and you need to check the boxes.

Now, if I were creating the checklist for you, I'd add a few things. I'd add a call every week, two weeks, or three weeks, to make sure that the customer is informed along the way during underwriting. This ensures that there's no buyer's remorse because they know everything is happening as planned.

I also want on my checklist when I'm going to deliver it when it comes back. On my checklist, I want to follow up after I deliver it to make sure they're happy with the purchase, and to see if they have any questions. Our studies show that retention is better for insurance if you call them three or four months after you deliver the policy. Then, there's the anniversary call on the life policy—you're getting the idea.

Every time there needs to be a touchpoint just on that product, you put it into the workflow. Do the other workflows stop? No. Let's start with focusing on one product. You may choose life, property, or auto. Focus on that workflow, and you'll see your retention swell.

Takeaway Questions:

1. Do you currently use checklists or flow sheets to track all new account activity? Who can you assign to create or refine these for your office?

____

____

____

____

____

2. How are you currently tracking the outstanding items on these checklists/workflows? Are they on the calendar as reminder events?

____

____

____

____

____

Actionable Item: Copy and paste the following onto your calendar!

Subject: Create Workflows for Your Products: Creating Continuity

Time Frame: 15 minutes

Notes: Ensure everyone in your office has an electronic and printed copy of all new account checklists/flow sheets.

Next Steps: Ensure each line item on the checklist/ flow sheet is turned into a calendar workflow item.

session 7

Under One Roof

Here's a big question: does every customer buy from you? No. It's a numbers game. But remember, your odds of selling more and selling longer-term sales are greater when you have a 360° view, and you're a Discussion Partner.

Maybe they didn't buy the auto from you; but that's not a lost sale. The customer is still yours. You're still the gateway. You need to follow up on that product, because you need to review it every year—even if they stayed where they were or went somewhere else for a service you couldn't provide.

With that being said, you always want to have all their insurance and financial services under one roof. That's how you get paid. Now, you're not putting the commission first, but you're getting the opportunity every time. There are no lost sales. Remember, we got to this point because we had great products, we offered great service; but it was all transactional, and it wasn't advice-based.

Your best customers have always been people who rely on you for advice; you're just flipping it upside down, and now you're focusing only on those folks that want advice. The transactions will come.

Your odds of selling more and selling longer-term sales are greater when you have a 360° view, and you're a Discussion Partner.

Practical Application: Create an Analytics Department

Here's an idea you can implement immediately. Again, it's all about assessment; it's all about tracking; it's all about benchmarking and analytics. You've heard this term: analytics. Create your own analytics department.

You do this by tracking all the people that came to you under the Discussion Partner model, and all the people you were doing a transaction with. If you're selling 20 of the 100 quotes in transactional selling, and you're losing 80, how much more profitable can you be with the Discussion Partner model—by giving them every option? How much bigger is the return on investment for your time and your money?

Takeaway Questions:

1. Is your office equipped to handle more business per household? What is your threshold?

____

____

____

____

____

2. Will your current infrastructure support a 10%, 20% or 30% increase in business? What practical steps can you take to make this a reality?

____

____

____

____

____

Actionable Item: Copy and paste the following onto your calendar!

Subject: Under One Roof: Creating an Insurance and Financial Services Superstore

Time Frame: 15 minutes

Notes: Assess your business to determine when changes to infrastructure will be needed to support growth.

Next Steps: Put a plan in place to add additional staff, equipment, square feet, etc. that aligns with the systematic growth of your firm.

Module 8:
A New Normal

introduction

You Need a Roadmap

What do we mean by "a new normal"? Everything is changing so quickly. You need to create an environment for the people you work with, so they have a roadmap when they come in every day. This means setting up systems and processes—scripts and continuity books that are refreshed and updated on a constant basis.

Most of us have had to create a business plan for one reason or another. A roadmap goes deeper—it's your day-to-day playbook. This section will be focusing on creating that roadmap. We're going to drill down and make something that helps you function more smoothly as an organization.

Takeaway Questions:

1. Do you currently have a roadmap for your business? If so, when was the last time you updated it? If not, what have you been using to stay on track?

2. What are some "destinations" you can already identify as an integral part of your organization's roadmap? Where do you want to go?

Actionable Item: Copy and paste the following onto your calendar!

Subject: You Need a Roadmap: Creating the Foundation

Time Frame: 15 minutes

Notes: Go online to review business roadmap and business plan templates. Use these as your guide to create your own personalized roadmap.

Next Steps: Create your roadmap section by section. Block time to work on this a few minutes daily until it is completed.

session 1

Be Prepared

To be prepared for the new normal, you need to do a real evaluation of everything. Nothing is more important than an evaluation of the Profit and Loss for your business—the P&L—the money.

There's also a P&L that needs to be done on *time*. We all know you can make more money if you have more time. Money you can make back; but time you can't get back. So, we're going to do two separate P&Ls to be more efficient with our time, and to make sure we're the most effective with everything we do.

Let's do the same for money. You want to line item everything that you have for expenses, and then put all the revenue and sources from which they came. You want to set goals and benchmarks as you go into the future. Why is a Profit and Loss so important to corporations, carriers, regions, states, and individual agencies? Because all businesses rely on Profit and Loss. They live and die by it. If you don't know where your biggest expenses and/or revenues come from, you can't properly plan!

I always like to use the example of a casino. How often does a casino do a Profit and Loss? Some people say every month; some people say every week; but it's every hour. Why? Because if they're going to lay money out on the table, they've got to know where they're at. They don't make an uninformed bet.

Our business is not a bet. Our business is to be counted on... if we count the money correctly. It's a numbers game, so you want to line item everything in the way of money: money coming in and money going out. At the end of the day, we're for profit.

All businesses rely on Profit and Loss. They live and die by it.

With that being said, part of your roadmap needs to be the amount of time that you spend in each area of your business. If you spend 60% of your time on servicing auto, but only 30% of your revenue is coming from auto, something needs to be adjusted. I can honestly say that, in my early years, I thought time would never end. I thought I'd have enough time to do everything. I thought, "I'll do that tomorrow." But life just doesn't work that way. You've got to do what you need to do today—and not just in your business life, in your personal life as well.

We all got into this business for three reasons: to make more money, to have more fun, and to have less stress in our lives. If you don't have all three of those things, you need to reassess your P&L, both for money and for time.

Practical Application: Outsource

Today, we're living in a world where you can get just about any information you want—and you can get most of it for free! I like to outsource everything that I can because there's an expense to things like payroll. I want the payroll to be for the customer, and so I outsource it along with social media, accounting, and legal. They're vendors; I don't pay payroll on those things, or the related expenses.

Remember, if you spend a dollar on payroll, the odds are you're spending an additional fifty-one cents for the benefit load: social security, work comp, health insurance, 401k... you get the idea. I'm going to outsource as much as I can. On the P&L side, if you're not going to outsource, find a good program that allows you to pay pennies on the dollar—or one you can get for free.

Takeaway Questions:

1. When was the last time you conducted a Profit and Loss (P&L) of your business finances? What about the time spent within your business?

____

____

____

____

____

2. How often do you compare your current P&L against your current goals? How do these align or misalign? Where are the biggest discrepancies?

____

____

____

____

____

Actionable Item: Copy and paste the following onto your calendar!

Subject: Be Prepared: P&L

Time Frame: 15 minutes

Notes: Run a current P&L of your business finances. Go down each line item and determine an estimated percentage of time spent in each of these areas of expense.

Next Steps: Do the same for revenue. Begin to systematically audit your P&L figures against your goals.

session 2

Have a Vision

Part of your roadmap needs to be having a real vision for your organization. That means you've got to sit down and figure out where you're going and where you want to be. If you're going to be a leader, you've got to have a vision. As it's stated, "Without vision, the people will perish."

You've got to have a pure statement that everybody can agree to; but you've got to live that vision and make it actionable.

If you want to grow your organization—whether there's two people, twenty people, two thousand, or twenty thousand—you've got to have a real, clear vision of where you're going. Otherwise, everybody gets lost. I would submit to you that you want to work on your vision every day. You've got to have a pure statement that everybody can agree to; but you've got to live that vision and make it actionable.

Practical Application: Solidify Your Agency Values

What are your agency values? That's the core of your vision: what you stand for. I love going into corporate offices, firms, or agencies and seeing them put their vision right out front for their customer to see.

What better time to retool your vision? You're going from being a transactional seller to a Discussion Partner—a real advisor. Why not put that as part of your vision, and let your clients know when they come through the door?

Takeaway Questions:

1. Do you currently have a pure statement (vision statement) for your business? If so, do you share this with your current team and clients?

____

____

____

____

____

2. What do you consider to be your top values that set you apart from your competition? Are these included in your pure statement?

____

____

____

____

____

Actionable Item: Copy and paste the following onto your calendar!

Subject: Have a Vision: Creating a Pure Statement

Time Frame: 15 minutes

Notes: Create or refine a pure statement that sums up the "why" of your business in a few sentences.

Next Steps: Display this throughout your office and have it become part of every client presentation.

session 3

Staff Development

Part of your roadmap needs to include the priority of staff development. We talked a lot about staff earlier, as well as the importance of hiring the right person, training, and ongoing development. Make investments—not just in money, but in time and resources—for your staff. Your clients are demanding more information, content, and delivery. So, your staff needs to offer more to your clients tomorrow than they do today.

What worked yesterday doesn't work today; and what works today won't work tomorrow. We know this to be true. So have a library of information; have resources they can go to in order to learn more. We've found that almost all staff we've encountered nationwide are eager to learn and grow. They tell us it builds their confidence, and they're proud of the knowledge they've gained. All leaders are readers, and you never want to stop learning about your product, how to deliver service, and how to communicate. You need to work on improving your skills every day, because the past does not equal the future.

You never want to stop learning about your product, how to deliver service, and how to communicate.

Practical Application: Invest in Your Staff

Have a percentage of your income be dedicated to learning—for you, and everyone on your team. We've studied growing distribution agency systems. The ones that are growing are staffing up and making investments of money and time into their staff.

You want to focus on spending the right amount of money. It could be 2% or 5%. Take the total budget, and block time for them to learn during working hours; to be able to go to conferences; to learn from other industries.

The skill set that's needed for tomorrow isn't just about product, or how to present product. It's about communicating, handling conflict, and learning things they don't know anything about today that they can apply in future situations. Invest in time and invest in money.

Takeaway Questions:

1. What is your current budget specifically for staff development? Why did you choose that percentage/amount?

____

____

____

____

____

2. Does the company (or companies) you represent offer sponsored or subsidized training opportunities for staff? These could be webinars, teleconferences, in person events, etc.

____

____

____

____

____

Actionable Item: Copy and paste the following onto your calendar!

Subject: Staff Development: Budgeting for Growth

Time Frame: 15 minutes

Notes: Determine a monetary and time budget for staff development (monthly, quarterly, annually) that works for your firm.

Next Steps: Get the training on the calendar now! Each person in your office should have some type of business development training on their calendar every month.

session 4

Retooling Your Database

Retooling your database is a necessary element for your roadmap. We've agreed that we have, or need to have, a CRM system. No matter how great or how deficient, we all know we haven't populated enough information into it. I've never met any organization or distribution system that can show me that they've populated 100% of the data they need.

We've been working on this for years. As an agent, I used to work on it. But as a consultant, here's my advice: everybody needs to double down on getting the information. I believe in retooling days. Stop everything and get the information. Don't have any appointments for one day; get on the phone, call your customers, and thank them for having business with your firm, agency, or carrier. Then say, "To better serve you, I need to get a little bit of information from you."

Then, go down the list and start populating: "When's your birthday? Who are your kids? Where do they go to school? How do I contact you? Ways to contact him. Ways to contact her. Ways to contact the kids. What are your favorite social media devices that you use? How can I contact you better? What type of policies do you have?"

I've never met any organization or distribution system that can show me that they've populated 100% of the data they need.

The more information I can get every time I touch my client—not just the first appointment, but throughout the journey of the relationship—the more effective a Discussion Partner I can be. Retooling your database must be one of your top priorities if you're going to transform to the Discussion Partner model.

Practical Application: The Retooling Day Kit

Here's a little nugget to help you with your retooling day: I've been doing thousands of these for years, helping carriers, agencies, and firms. I've got a kit I can send you. It will start you on the process, and you can refine it to fit your needs and your customers' needs.

Email me at support@korsgaden.com, and I'll send it to you, so you can start building your own personalized system.

Takeaway Questions:

1. Do you currently have all the information needed for every one of your current clients?

____

____

____

____

____

2. When was the last time you called your client to just say "thank you" for doing business with your firm? How can you begin to integrate this into your daily and weekly routines?

____

____

____

____

____

Actionable Item: Copy and paste the following onto your calendar!

Subject: Retooling the Database: Set the Date

Time Frame: 15 minutes

Notes: Get a date on the calendar to do a retooling day in your office.

Next Steps: Continue to schedule retooling days until everyone in your book of business has been contacted (monthly, bi-monthly, quarterly, etc.).

session 5

Client Retention

There's a lot of things you're going to put into your roadmap that I didn't bring up here, because we want to get right to the point in order to help you get the process started. But retention is a crucial piece. If we write a single policy household/business, and we lose it six months later—or even six years later—we pretty much lost a client. Under the Discussion Partner model, we never lose a client if we focus on being the information that they need on every product and service.

We focus on the customer, not the transaction.

As the market changes, the retention of the client really doesn't change. What I want you to think about today is how you're going to retain the relationship—not the policy or the coverage. The relationship is based on advice. Remember, Discussion Partner clients don't want to be sold, and they don't want to be told. They want to have a discussion. They want to make the decision that's best for them and their family. With that being said, we focus on the customer, not the transaction.

Practical Application: Find Out Your Competitors' Retention Rates

It doesn't matter what carrier you represent—you need to look at the top retention of all your competitors. This is information you can get. When you find out what the retention is, yours should be the same or better, because you're not focusing on the product; you're focusing on the customer.

Takeaway Questions:

1. What is your current retention ratio for each product and service you offer?

____

____

____

____

____

2. What area(s) need the most attention? Create a plan to improve retention by 1%, 3%, 5%, etc., over the next twelve-months.

____

____

____

____

____

Actionable Item: Copy and paste the following onto your calendar!

Subject: Client Retention: Increasing Retention

Time Frame: 15 minutes

Notes: Pull a report of your current retention numbers. Set goals to increase these based on your growth objectives.

Next Steps: Audit monthly to ensure you are hitting your goals.

closing

Becoming a Discussion Partner

I would like to thank you for your time, commitment, and monetary investment into The Discussion Partner Program. All the programs and systems presented to you in these videos, and in the corresponding workbook, are tried and true. Not only did I use them when I was a practicing agency firm owner, but they have been adapted in thousands of agency firms worldwide.

I recognize that you have received an abundance of information and actionable items. Don't allow yourself to become overwhelmed. Remember, the best way to eat an elephant is one bite at a time! It is far better to have 2 – 3 systems that you are carrying out consistently than 10 you are not. The key is to start!

You are not alone on this journey. If me, or my team, can help you anywhere along the way, please reach out to us. Again, our email is support@korsgaden.com, or you can call us at 800-524-6390. Congratulations on taking the first step in becoming a successful Discussion Partner Operation! May you achieve all the success you pursue!